# AROUND THE
# KITCHEN TABLE
## *Lancashire Childhood*

*GB in the kitchen yard at 147, Leam Terrace.*

# AROUND THE
# KITCHEN TABLE

## *A Lancashire Childhood*

*Gertrude Bark*

*Edited by Diana Good*

BREWIN BOOKS

**09497233**

First published by Brewin Books Ltd
Studley, Warwickshire B80 7LG in 2004
www.brewinbooks.com

ISBN 1 85858 249 0

The moral right of the author has been asserted.

British Library Cataloguing in Publication Data
A Catalogue record for this book is available
from the British Library.

Typeset in Times
Printed in Great Britain by
Alden Press Limited

# ACKNOWLEDGEMENTS

GB wrote the book by dictating the stories about the recipes to friends who then wrote up and typed the script. I participated in the dictating phase and edited the book later. Many thanks are owed to Katherine Jenkins and John Brassington who took virtually all the dictation, my mother, Valerie Hope, who did the typing and for all her help, Angela Cameron, Chairman of the Gertrude Bark Memorial Bursary Trust, for her support, Kate Kellaway for her good and kind advice, Katherine Webb for all her IT skills and correspondence, my father, Michael Hope for his 1960's photographs of Leigh, Lancashire, where his mother and GB first met at nursery school which supplement GB's original photographs, my husband, Alex for his patience, affection and help on all fronts and finally my girls, Kate, Harriet, Frances and Gloria, for their enthusiasm when listening to me reading the book out loud. GB knew only Kate, but she urged me to have more, and I did.

As GB would say, "Ever onwards"!

*Diana Good*

*GB aged about 10 years.*

*"The whole world aglow
again after so long,
so very long!"*

# INTRODUCTION

I always knew her as GB. Gertrude Bark didn't like her Christian name and was always irritated in later years when the Vicar, in avuncular and rather patronising tones, called her "Gertrude". Hence "GB".

GB was a smallish person with a pretty oval shaped face, very bright eyes and a lovely voice. I look at the photographs we have of her and I see the same person in each of the pictures: a 10 year old in a pretty white dress; a nurse in Manchester during the First World War; and an 80 year old in her kitchen with a mischievous look. I remember GB telling me, when she was in her 90s, that she felt exactly the same inside as she did when she was 16. Perhaps this is why all age groups got on so well with her.

If I summon GB up in my mind I think of her voice, her lively eyes and her large hands which were gnarled with arthritis but were always warm, generous and active. I was very aware of her hands and I can see them now cooking, welcoming people into the house and playing the piano (which she did extremely well on her grand piano, duets galore).

She was born in 1896 in Leigh, Lancashire, the only daughter of William Smith, Secretary of the Bedford Colliery, and his wife Gertrude France. In her late 20s GB moved from Leigh to Leamington Spa to be married and so Gertrude Smith became Gertrude Bark but her thoughts always went back to her first coal mining home and the miners for whom she had a great affection.

It was GB's pleasure in thinking about her childhood that prompted her to do something about the recipe book which her parents had started as newly weds. Although GB liked cooking, it was not the food which was the important aspect of a meal, but the talk which went with it and so it was with the recipes. For GB each recipe conjured up a memory of a place or event or friendship. As a very old lady and almost bedridden in an old people's home, GB would read a recipe out and then talk about the person or story which that particular recipe evoked. Friends would note down or tape what GB said and the warmth of her childhood came alive in her voice and eyes. From the way that she talked, it was clear that her home was a very happy one and that life was rich with talk, reading, music and fun.

Gertrude France and William Smith were married in the late 1890s. GB's father ("Pal" as she called him) was the cashier and bookkeeper at Bedford Colliery in Leigh. William Smith first met Gertrude France when he went to collect payment for the coal bills from the milliner's shop where she worked. Together they noted down recipes in an old exercise book. Initially William took dictation for the recipes from his young wife often bemused by her cook's shorthand expressions. Later on neighbours and friends passed on recipes when they came to talk in the kitchen and parlour. GB also made notes; initially as a child and later when she was herself a mother right through to the Second World War.

The recipes appear in chronological order in the way the recipes were written over the years and so are "higgledy-piggledy" as GB explains. What this means is that we can see the changing times of the recipes from the 1890s when William Smith noted down "Sponge Cake" alongside "Furniture

*Portrait of William Smith - known to GB as 'Pal'.*

Paste" to the simple and economic recipes of the First World War, then the introduction of foreign dishes learned at cookery classes between the wars, and finishing with the very last recipe for Bee Syrup in 1945.

And so we learn about Grandma's Raised Pies which she brought out at midnight on New Year's Eve as "all the bells of heaven were bursting from the quiet town" and of much loved Cousin Dick who in 1916 wrote from the trenches to GB (then a nurse) imagining "arriving during some starshine night in Manchester all the way from the trenches and be sure to have a chunk of your chocolate cake in your pocket for me". But Cousin Dick never did come back.

Of course, none of us today knew GB in her youth so the recipe book opens that up and allows us to imagine her "coal mining cotton spinning" Leigh at the turn of the 20th Century. To us GB was the great friend who lived at 147, Leam Terrace, an English teacher at Feldon boys' school in Leamington Spa into her 70s, someone with a huge knowledge of theatre and literature, a pianist, and a wonderful talker.

She was a remarkable woman: an ordinary person from an ordinary background but someone with an exceptional talent for enthusing others and bringing the best out of everyone she met. Her real gift was the power to encourage and stimulate others, especially the young. She loved to find out about people and wherever she went people would talk to GB. When she was older and couldn't walk for long, we used to leave her for a while to rest on a park bench or seat and on return we would find GB in deep discussion and laughing with someone – a small child, a lumpish teenager or an old gentleman.

She was wonderful company. Being with her was so invigorating that you felt cleverer, wittier and more alive. If when talking one paused or hesitated, she would lean forward, eyes sparkling and say "Go on, go on, I want to hear more". Most of all we had fun or "larks "as GB would say. She would jump off a swing (even at the age of 78), stride back from tea in Warwick in the frosty dark, fly kites on the Burton Dassett hills and play funny tunes on the piano. She had hundreds of friends, many of them two or three generations younger than herself.

GB taught English until she was in her 70s and huge numbers of her old boys kept in touch with her. It is clear that she was able to command and enthral a class of boys just by a look and a raised eyebrow. After her funeral many of these old boys and friends wrote down what had made her special to them. I can recognise my GB in each of these brief comments. "GB could spot from a mile off those of us who felt we had little hope. By sharing her love of literature and the arts she gave me the power to escape the painful realities that awaited me at home at the end of the day", "It was thanks to her that the world of books was opened up for me. That sense of wonder never went away" and "I can see her now: she would stand in the doorway looking me directly in the eye and with that quizzical smile she would give me her judgement."

My family friendship with GB started two generations before me. She went to nursery school with my grandmother and great aunt. My father used to spend holidays there as a boy and he took my mother to meet GB before he proposed just as I later sought GB's approval before I married my husband.

A visit to 147, Leam Terrace was always a treat. I remember finishing my O levels, walking out and going straight to the station to catch a train to Leamington Spa. Walking from the station in the sunshine I was hailed by GB from an old boy's car (there were many of these young "old boys" who came from the school she had taught at). They swept me off to see "Macbeth" at Stratford and it was thrilling. That night we talked until four in the morning and laughed with tears in our eyes over her copy of David Garrick's version of the play which he had rewritten to give himself a better death scene than Shakespeare had devised, with much staggering and scope for melodramatic death throes. Time was never an object at 147 so to talk until 4 am was not unusual nor was having lunch at 6pm or breakfast at noon. Time would just disappear as talk or music or picking damsons in the garden took over.

I loved 147 – the rooms full of books and pictures, model boats, stuffed animals, treasured objects such as GB's old miners' lamps and old toys – the glorious chaos of it with shelves, glass cases and drawers full of interest and GB's past. For me 147 was full of music and books and talk for happy hours on end. For GB it was more of a struggle as the house was far too much for her to maintain and it was a constant battle to make ends meet and to stay the inevitable decay and collapse of roof, window frames and paintwork, whilst also rescuing the garden from disappearing under weeds and brambles. As a result GB always turned visits into an opportunity to tackle some aspect of the house or the garden and we would paint the kitchen or turn out the shed or prune the pear tree but it was always fun and we would break for tea and coffee and more talk, often and often.

Arriving at 147 involved walking up the path past the old oak tree (which blew down in a storm and was then turned into a sturdy fireside chair) and between the overgrown holly bushes. When I visited with my husband in our first car, GB liked the idea of us driving up to the front door as if the path were a drive but even in our very small Citroen Diane this was quite a feat. Then there was the wait at the big black front door with its large brass knocker, sometimes a very long wait when GB was in the kitchen or the garden and couldn't hear the doorbell or the knocker. Finally GB would open the door, hands and elbows covered in flour. With sparkling eyes GB would explain that she was making scones and that there was just time to eat them before going to Stratford for a poetry reading.

Through the dark hallway past the big sideboard where lodgers would leave a note indicating whether they were "in" or "out" and where GB had every possible order for the milkman ready written out ("3 pints, one cream, 6 eggs" or "2 pints" or "no milk today" etc). Past the large high ceilinged and rather gloomy front rooms to the back of the house where GB in later years had turned the dining room into her bedroom and the servants scullery into a very small and cosy back parlour/study/dining room to which we would all retreat from the chill in the corridors. Here there was warmth and sunshine and the dining table was crammed into the room and always covered with books and letters, a huge typewriter and other writing materials. These would be swept aside to make room for pork pies, tomatoes, a mug of soup and a glass of sherry.

It was a lovely room to sit in with views out over the walled garden with overgrown roses, damson, pear and apple trees and vegetable garden full of beans and tomatoes, lettuces, potatoes and carrots. All the produce would be taken into the kitchen where pears would be bottled and apples would be laid out in drawers only to be found months later wizened with age.

The kitchen was an extraordinary place. A large room with very high ceilings, not cosy and always cold with only a small window out onto the yard. It was the most crowded kitchen I have ever seen with pots and pans on every surface, old jam jars labelled "Cold tea – good for cuts", saucepans in which yoghurt was curdling, jugs with gauze tops weighted down with beads protecting who-knew-what underneath. The photograph of GB in her kitchen in her 80s) gives some impression of the chaos. Her notes on the back of the photo read " Siberia. Even the wine bottles are wrapped. Note shining cooker! Object above is a pan strainer, not a fillet of plaice." In the photo GB is wearing Jean Simmons' coat. (One of GB's old boys went into the theatre and introduced her to a number of film stars and actors including Jean Simmons who was concerned about how cold it was at 147 so she gave GB her sheepskin coat to keep warm.)

The pride of her kitchen were the cupboards which her father had made of sturdy oak with huge deep drawers full of the aged collection of battered dishes and saucepans with wobbly handles which her mother had used before her. Pastry was rolled out on her father's dresser once jars of salted beans, bottled pears and homemade wine had been moved out of the way. The food which GB produced in this cluttered and chaotic kitchen was always delicious and although many of the recipes in the book were used, the ones I remember best were the scones and Cousin Dick's chocolate cake. The food always played second fiddle to talk though. GB always said that she would never leave anything she was enjoying in order to cook, hence the very odd timing of many meals.

In going through the book, it has been a great joy to hear GB's voice telling the stories of the recipes. GB loved Lancastrian speech and she was very anxious that no one should change the words in the book and I have not. What I have done, though, in some places is to group together the stories that relate to a particular person. I hope that GB would approve.

*Diana Good*

*GB in the kitchen at 147 Leam Terrace, New Year 1977, wearing the coat given to her by the film star Jean Simmons, with coffee pot. GB's notes on the back read: "Siberia – even the wine bottles are wrapped. What Michael Hope calls a "workaday backdrop". Note shining cooker! Object above is a pan strainer not a fillet of plaice. Coffee pot made by grandson of Bernard Leach (John Leach), Somerset."*

Notes by friends and old boys:

"Gertrude Bark was a wonderful lady whose memory is fixed in the hearts and minds of those who knew her. What a motley company still call themselves her family, friends, her pupils: actors, artists, musicians, writers, neighbours, tradespeople, even a film star or two. A whole network of relationships intersected at her home, 147 Leam Terrace."(John Brassington)

"GB could spot from a mile off those of us who felt we had little hope. By sharing her love of literature and the arts she gave me the power to escape the painful realities that awaited me at home at the end of the day. For the first time I felt trusted; and she gave me my first responsibility, a leading role in her beloved school play. With her patience, guidance, encouragement and love she gave me an identity, a purpose, self respect... she gave me life." (David Warner)

"Many teachers pretend to know and will then enforce what is good for their pupils, but few can persuade those same pupils into the adventure which is true education."(John Brassington)

"It was thanks to her that the world of books was opened up for me. That sense of wonder never went away. She used to get cross with herself when she couldn't quote the line she wanted exactly, when she wanted it. In fact she'd forgotten more about Shakespeare than I will ever know, but she would never accept that. She always gave me credit for being as intelligent as she was."(Huw Mordecai)

"147 Leam Terrace was really a museum with its pictures, books, models, its grand piano and fine furniture, its items of interest everywhere, reflecting her life and interests. There she lived, absorbed in her activities, always enthusiastic and with that twinkle in her eye, even in the later days of illness, when she seemed confined to one room, keeping warm with her shawl-and always writing,"(Robin Chapman)

" I came into contact with GB at the Loft Theatre, of which she had been a founder member and Vice President. Whenever I acted there she would attend a performance and always made her way to the dressing room after the show. I can see her now: she would stand in the doorway looking me directly in the eye and with that quizzical smile she would give me her judgement. Whatever she said was always relevant, informed and crammed with the wisdom of experience. When I went to the Edinburgh Festival in Hamlet, there was a hand made card waiting in the dressing room on the first night from GB. Inside were some of the lines I was to speak as Polonius:

> "This above all: to thine own self be true,
> And it must follow, as the night the day,
> Thou can'st not then be false to any man."

How well GB lived by these guidelines!" (David Biddle)

*GB's father in the doorway of 147 with Bill, GB's son.*

# THE RECIPE BOOK: FORETASTE

You can see straight away where this book came from - coal dust smudged all the way through, some pages very black, colliers - a lifetime in this small exercise book.

What sort of place were these recipes living in from 1890 onwards? Coal mining, cotton spinning, silk weaving Leigh with the Manchester Ship Canal and barges passing through by cottages: among them "Jones's Buildings" on a round name plate over the two doors of two joint houses, where my father was born in 1864.

There was a literary society in Leigh which included a drama section, given to acting J.M. Barrie, Bernard Shaw and others; and more than one enthusiastic choir - church and town: one conducted by my eldest uncle where colliers and tradesmen sang mainly oratorios with full hearts and voices; another patronised by the more professional types and aristocratically snobbishly select - I use the word advisedly.

There were snobs among my uncle's choir too, vocally scornful of their moneyed and perhaps slightly more professional or academic brethren of the

*"Jones's Buildings: William Smith was born here in 1864."*

rival group (lawyers and doctors, librarians, schoolmasters, mill owners and their women folk). "Them queer things they call part-songs or summat - no more music in 'em than old Jack Scholfield's barrel organ!" Thus my friend, coal miner Jim.

Jim once brought me home from my wandering almost up to the pit-head, across a field or two and along the colliery's single line railway when I was on my way to meet my father walking home to his Mecca - the red blind to the window where my mother awaited him at day's end. I must have been about 4 or 5 years old then, and I remember hanging on to Jim's coally hand and can still remember the safe, comfortable smell of his trousers and the clanking of his tea cans at his belt as I trudged along with him far above me. I remember too the firmness and severity of his rebuke on delivering me to my mother at our yard gate. "She was welly up t'pit, Mrs.Smith. You've no right lettin' this lass o' yourn wander on her own, even i' daylight - and keep better watch on 'er." And my mother, "But she was all right, Jim, and thank you for bringing her back." "It shouldn't 'appen", clipped Jim at my mother, I still hanging on the coally hand. "Thank you, Jim - I know you're right; but with all you about....". "I know.", Jim turned to go, "Only it was a bit out o' 'er way; watch t' little lass a bit. She fears nowt!"

This was the sort who disappeared years later into the Great War. Jim had said, my father told me, when he was too old for war but still joined the army, "I'm agoing, Will - I can't stand this German Kaiser fellow and 'is 'me and my God' any longer." Dear Jim - dear, kind Jim - I am thankful I grew up among such as he, whom I trusted and never had cause to doubt.

There were, as I've said, many groups of so-called educational factions, some merely experimental and of brief existence - dwindling before they'd fully grown, like the foreign language classes at night school!

The Public Co-operative Library was different. It flourished as the co-operative commercialism flourished from the Blatchford Victorian Days; it saw my father and me most Friday evenings in the Co-op Reading Room, wallowing through my early teens and the 1914-18 war in such splendid adventuring as the Strand Magazine and the Socialist Weekly, "The Clarion" (now defunct with the upsurge of the misnamed Labour Party).

My mother's family were Tories - true blue, in days when Red and Blue were the only colours sported during elections. That was called "politics", and woe betide those who dared show the Tory rosette in our part of my industrial town in the Lancashire coal and cotton area. In 1900, in such "election fevers" as swelled then, it was not a deeply thought out reasonableness, but a wild, strongly biased human urge. I heard the same kind of verdict hurled against the influx of Irish in my youth. "An Irishman?

Oh! - 'eave 'alf a brick at 'im!" I never could see reason in that. We had so many Irish friends, known and guessed at. Great fighters among themselves: the short terraces near the pub agog with fury and glorious Irish imprecations and bloody blows, til suddenly Father Donnelly appeared with his shillelagh from the vicinity of St. Joseph's Roman Catholic Church. The narrow street echoed with the names Father Donnelly shouted as he stood; the street cleared as by magic and there was peace. Stirring times!

I remember being swept at a gallop from a Platt Fields open-air meeting where Keir Hardy held forth from a lorry 'til mounted police stampeded into the arena, and my parents seized me and we fled. We got over a gate just in time.

Life was very pleasant, even during a strike threatening serious riots and horrible bloodshed. A muster of soldiery, Royal Fusiliers no less, came down to keep order among "those miners and people". And within a week their regimental band came in full force, and we had military tattoos on the market place and gloriously efficient music. The bandmaster was billeted onto my Aunt - wonderful fortune. There were no riots. The soldiery were billeted in one of the schools - the council school - and life was a holiday of friendships, many long lasting.

About the strike again. On this particular winter day then, men, women and children came to the wharf with bassinets and wheelbarrows and buckets and baskets, and filled up with happy coal. It was a merry party. I went across a little field and took photographs of it with my new 5 shilling box Kodak (incidentally, in the Second World War madness, I sent it out to my elder son training with the R.A.F. in South Africa about forty years later. It did good service.) There was no enmity on that winter afternoon - when the strikers and their entourage were filling up from the wagons. "We can't have all these women and young uns starved wi' cold, this weather, can we, Will? Can you do summat about it?" said old John Speakman. This to my father. And of course he could - authorised like that - and did.

I remember being warned by some fussy well wishers to keep away - my father's, "It'll be all right, love - you're not frightened." It hadn't dawned on me to be - me and my new camera! And Tom and Jo and the rest: part of my life. One man - I knew them all - called out to me from a 10 ton wagon, "Wait a minute, lass", and he fixed his cap and sat smartly on the edge – "Now. See I get one, don't forget!" I had that snapshot among my treasures more than seventy years and two world wars later.

And when I married and moved - an exile – "a purr" of real, used miners' lamps went with me - their wedding present to me. Those men, the families shall have a book to themselves if I can last out.

These were the sort of men who asked my father: "What does 'er want for 'er weddin'?" My father, nearer to tears than I'd ever believed, asked me. I said, "A real miner's lamp - one they've used in the pit, not a shop new one." And my father told me that when he told them what I'd said I wanted, coal black Tom (family of five youngsters of his own) said without hesitation, "'Er can't have one - 'Er mun have a purr!" So I did: one old polished brass, the other metal cleaned, colga oil and wick in both, ready for use. I went down to the wharf and caught Jo and Tom (buddies) on their way home from t' pit at shift's end, and thanked them and them all. "Think nowt on it, lass," Jo said, "the'art welcome - eh Tom?" "Will Smith's lass? - aye, 'er's that. Dun ye like it, love? It were mine". A

*Shaft of Bickershaw Colliery (Leigh's last coal mine) by dawn's early light.*

hand gripped. And no more. That was just before 1923. The first Great War had intervened. The strike long past, (nearly twenty years) - a different world; empty of the old, friendly accepted security - of the old loyalty, wide-cast among unlike, and unlikely to late twentieth century eyes. Now we do not have a world where children need not fear.

There was, to continue the picture, much drinking of cheap beer, much drunkenness therefore. (It used to be said, a collier had three hobbies- women (i.e. wives), whippets and beer.) I have walked on an early spring evening from a tea with my grandparents in the town bakery not far from the Church of England parish church, with my mother linking arms with a not-quite-too-drunk-to-walk collier, chatting to him and eliciting unintelligible replies (understandable to her) and, still walking, bidding "Good Night - we're all right, Officer" to a well-known bobby who might otherwise have smelt a likely prisoner.

I was more than once on her other side on this sort of expedition, but not once was my mother stayed, or questions asked. Only a still, blue figure in the twilight, (pubs were open early, perhaps too early, in those days) and a recognisable voice calling, "Good night, Mrs. Smith!" as we wobbled along.

She knew both sides. Many times has she brought out one of the men from a pub's beer-swilling party. She knew what his family went through of misery and want, and too well she knew why. And she would tell him what she knew, quietly, and why. And he came out to her. I don't say he was a changed man immediately but there seems to have been no ill feeling on either side, ever.

She once mopped up a bleeding collier with the same calm, kindly purpose. He had fallen head first into the road by our house from the back of his empty coal cart senseless from drink, after his delivery duty at some house not far away. I hovered and I was told to fetch a jug of water and not drop it. All went well. I stood and watched her empty into the road the bloody bowl she had run out with and refill it from my jug and mop his head. A passing collier, going home at the end of his shift, crossed the road; "I'll see him right, Mrs. Smith. He's not hurt. Drunken men fall easy, you know. I know where he lives - not far. Horse alright?" Another group came up the street. "We've seen 'im afore", they laughed. Horse and cart were taken, without question, the quarter mile to the colliery wharf. All was calm, uneventful, normal life, as normal a happening as any in life, as far as I knew. It was beginning to grow darker - still light enough to see and hear the "good nights" as we took in the jug and basin and lit the gas lamps in the kitchen and then to our home, with its red blind, for my father's joyful welcome home at the close of this part of his working day. My father often used to spend many evening hours, after his six o'clock tea, at his desk, checking accounts for the colliery business. Then came the life we loved before bed in that happy, working home.

One of the miners was a "special" of mine and I called him 'Rosy Lee'. Rosy had a family of handsome girls, and lived a few doors higher up our street, next to the alley. Once, when I was bedfast with one of my 'bad throats', Rosy arrived at our door with a black kitten for me, "an I'll tek it upstairs to her," he said to my mother as she let him in. "It'll do her a world o' good, I know 'er wanted a black 'un", as he made for the stairs, not waiting, nor expecting remonstrance. Off came his great boots, neatly placed on the bottom step, my mother told me, and up and in to me. (I was about 6 years old and given to no ailments but sore throats - imperfectly operated tonsils two years before and a menace until middle-age). "How's that?" said Mr. Lee, coal miner, and held up in his great scarred hands a wonderland of a black kitten - "That's aw reet? Feel better now, love?" And I croaked, "O Rosy!" He smiled on me and out he went, my kitten burbling, a quiet little heap on my bed. I touched her and I heard him go down the stairs. I heard his kind voice say to my mother, "'er'll be aw reet now, and don't you worry, Misses Willim, 'ers aw reet now." Then my mother, "Thank you, Rosy, thank you!" The front door closed - I think I must have slept. Dear Rosy; dear, kind Rosy. When I woke, there stood my mother with a warm flannel bandage for my throat in her quiet hands. Rosy's kitten was still there, by my side. I felt her warm comforting fur - so soft, so soft. Rosy, Rosy! - and my mum. In a dream, I saw my father come, silent, in. He put his arm round my mother, and she burst into sudden tears. I felt well and happy again, and very, very safe. A wonderful world. Sleep.

*Monday morning back street conversation.*

In the early 1890's or towards the end of the 1880's my father-to-be was preparing to marry his Gertrude France, milliner, at the shop where he called to be paid his firm's coal bills. His employer and rescuer advised him to embark on building another pair of houses tacked on to the above dark brick twins but not with bay windows. He offered to lend the money needed and William was to pay it back. William did. I still have the builder's accounts. William's wages were not large. He was the colliery secretary and had lodged in the long terrace at the other ("top") end of the street.

Two short facing lines of small terraced cottages (so-called 'workmen's') turned across our street towards the main town at a general shop where my mother bought vegetables and the neighbouring children spent their Saturday penny (if they had one) on Lemon Kali, with a tiny tin spoon from a brittle wooden container or a stick of liquorice, (not my choice though). I remember heaving twenty pounds of potatoes down to our house from this same shop, and my mother's horror on my arrival. She had sent me for two pounds - to give my five year old boundless energy something to do! Old Mrs. Jackson said, "Your mother never has less than a score. You should know *that!*" And weighed them out. I didn't know, but dragged them home in a sack!

Our Recipe House, where my father and mother made their home when they were married in 1890, was very like many of the other smaller, semi-detached houses in the town - quite unpretentious. It was one of two identical but reversed, door to door, the last in a varied, one-sided street of pairs leading from twenty or so at the top. All had bay windows of a uniform dark grey-blue brick and separated from homes that came a bit later, by an alley to their alleyed back doors. These later houses were solid, two to three bedroomed houses - kitchen and parlours. Then came progress, perhaps? A reversed pair, proclaiming its later vintage and slightly wider than the terrace pairs, of red brick, stone mullions, short path of two strides to front doors, walled garden (three foot high wall) with about three yards by one yard of

*"The shop across the road from Jones's building."*

garden, iron gate, and railings round top of wall, and a general air of being owner-occupied. Comfortable family dwellings.

Before the next pair (in darker brick, with bay windows again, and a few steps up to the front door) came another paved alley, wide enough to accommodate a coal cart and horse, as they passed the sides and side gates of the yards of these well-built erections. Again there were narrow, low-walled gardens, usually with persevering, coally green shrubs and ornamental, neat iron surmounts along the walls and possessively gated, up *one* step at this point, from the street on to the little path.

Ours was the last house in the street, number 36 Guest Street, in the Bedford area of Leigh where the colliery and cotton mills were. A high brick wall stretched out along all the opposite side, from the town at the top to the open fields at the bottom and the road to the colliery. Just beyond Shaw's brewery behind the high brick wall was Courtaulds, one-time Huguenot émigrés from France. Then on our side, Jones's affluent cotton mill behind us, blew little soft bits of cotton waste through one or other of our open back windows.

An organ builder - Heaven be praised! - played in an erection at the end of the alley where I stood and listened, entranced. Beyond our back yard was a square of grassy field where we played, and on cold winter days we warmed our frozen hands and bottoms on the hot brick, black painted gable of the house - our kitchen fire was on the other side. Comfort, safety forever!

*"Guest Street and the long brick wall of Shaw's brewery."*

Across the field ran a sluggish brook - it was not for wading in - too many old tins and broken bottles but we loved to cross it by the high-walled bridge and walk along the top to the coal wharf on the other side, where the check weighman's head popped up and down at his office window and wagons and carts were unloaded and loaded, and we could talk to our friends, drivers and loaders and horses, and be ever joyful.

My father, with old Speakman's connivance (he owned the colliery, and my father had become, on a token sort of wage, a sort of secretary manager by now), organised wagon-loads of coal to be trundled by our colliery engine - "the Bedford" she was called. I used to ride on the Bedford with the driver, all shining brass work and comforting coal smells between wharf and Pit.

Tommy Cooper, the check weighman, always kept his Ready Reckonner on the shelf under his desk at the wharf. He consulted it for every calculation and returned it to its place. It was never left out on the desk for easy access. This caused Father great amusement - things wouldn't have been the same without Tommy and his Ready Reckonner.

Once Tommy and his sister went on a day trip to Boulogne, his one trip abroad. After his return he came to our door and handed my mother a small parcel saying, "This is a present for Gertie. It's a brooch, and it says 'Boo-log-ney soo-er Mer' on it. Thought she would like it because she speaks French and you know *all* the children speak French over there."

*Bedford Colliery (also known as Speakman's Pit).*

When any money was paid in for coal on a Friday, after the bank closed, Tommy would bring it to my father to look after for the weekend. Father hid it behind a panel under the bath. One Sunday evening we were gone for a walk instead of going to church. When we returned, Father's desk in the kitchen was streaming with ink - the thief had sorted through Father's things and knocked the inkwell over. Father shot upstairs to the bathroom and saw that his hiding place was still secure. "It's all right Mother!" he called. That was all he worried about. The thief had climbed in through the bathroom window and walked straight past it! Mother's housekeeping purse had gone, that was all. And my Dr.Barnardo's collecting box was broken open but it had just been emptied a week before. The black mouth mark on the milk jug was the only trademark left behind! This theft was linked with that of a hotpot from a nearby house, which had been finished with a 'borrowed' spoon and left near our back wall and which pointed to the fact of both thefts being the work of the same person.

That night Bob, one of the brick kiln men, knocked on the door and said "I'll be back wi' two of me dogs, Will" - and he was. Two great bloodhounds which he bred. He left these in our back yard for that night and several subsequent ones. I watched them from my bedroom window pace the yard all night in the moonlight. Grandma's typical comment was "If you'd gone to church, it wouldn't have happened".

*"My mother, grandmother, Aunt Jane and my father at the gate of 36 Guest Street."*

Our house had a garden gate, two or three stones as a path and two stone steps up to the front door. A few years later on, when they had saved enough, a vestibule with a stained-glass window in the inner door, was added, and beyond it a lobby leading upstairs. At the top of the stairs one passed through an arch, along a short corridor past the bathroom to the left, and at the end of the passage into a third bedroom overlooking the adjacent cotton mill. This was really my father's room, where he made and mended stools of all sizes and any other furniture needed for the home. There were his punchball and boxing gloves and long stick (a form of fencing) which he also taught me.

At the top of the stairs just in front of the arch, you turned sharp left on your tracks up five steps onto the top landing, on the right a door into what became, ten years later, my bedroom. And at the end of the short landing, past a chest of drawers, the door into my parents' larger bedroom with two windows overlooking the street and beyond a long brick wall - Shaw's brewery. Under my parents' room was the parlour, under my room was the kitchen-living room, under the bathroom was the scullery, under my father's workroom was the wash house with my swing in the doorway into the yard. I came 'home' on a visit long years after I had married and exiled into Warwickshire, and walked round to the old early home, 36 Guest Street. I ventured to push open the familiar yard gate and suddenly a pretty

*View over South Lancashire plain from near Bottom 'oth' Moor, Bolton.*

face emerged from the old scullery door. "Do come in! Did you want the lavatory?" "Thank you, no. I used to live here long ago ......" "Oh! Are you Gertie Smith? Come in! I'm Harry Hilton's daughter - my husband's here. Do come in!"

Harry Hilton! Whose mother used to come to help mine (never in good health, though always energetic) after I was born forty years and more before: he went on errands to the shops for my mother, and played with me such games as 'shop', with stones and bunches of grass, dandelions or colt's foot from the adjacent field and railway line (i.e. "flowers"), and tea parties. Harry Hilton! And "Hilty", dead years gone by, who scrubbed the front door steps and whitened them, and bore me - just old enough to toddle - on her back. Dear, patient Hilty with her wild, wild husband and too large a family, and the courage of a quiet lion. Oh Hilty! Small and fierce and kind! You were our life. We all loved you, dearly. And here was your grand-daughter. "Now", she said. "You can tell us what the holes are in the wash house doorway. My father wasn't sure." The swing! The world aglow again after so long, so very long!

# THE BEGINNING OF THE BOOK

I don't know of any written recipes my mother collected before she was married. She must have done her share of the cooking. She (Gertrude) was the second of a family of five. Born in 1864, the second half of the nineteenth century was drawing on, and the next girl was to come ten years later, very much my mother's baby. Two brothers came between them: Richard (my mother's favourite) and Seth.

The eldest of the family, brother Ellis, was a musician - organist and choirmaster of Hindley Church, chosen out of a group of older men at the age of fifteen. There was no money in that united, quiet-living, church-going, merry family, for the music lessons he needed. School fees were a penny a week at the Church School, where Grandmother's sister, Martha, was Headmistress. (I still have the gold and garnet brooch the parents gave her when she retired in 1896; and I have the rackety hand bell she rang three times a day to call the children in to school.) But Ellis had to have music lessons.

Grandfather was poorlyish, tubercular, short of breath, handsome, tall with a white beard softly combed over his chest, and blue, humorous eyes we children could not resist. We liked Grandma too, but she was always sitting down, and she didn't make us laugh or play dominoes or tell tales as Grandpa did. And he played the violin. He was a silk spinner in his early days. He was lovely to look at, and we loved Grandpa.

Anyway, Uncle Ellis had to have music lessons. So, my mother left school at fourteen and was led into the silk mill owned by Grandpa's buddy (though they went to different churches). He was a Wesleyan. Grandpa was a warden at his church: C. of E., St Mary the Virgin, 15th century like the old Grammar School by the church gate.

Mother went to the silk mill with Aunt Jane - most beloved, Grandma's youngest sister who never married, tho'

*Ellis France (Uncle Ellis who "had to have piano lessons").*

19

she was once engaged to the curate of the parish church. She was very pretty and sparkly - just right for us children. Long after this time (we weren't born then of course) she used to take us children on holidays to the sea to stay with her friend who ran a boarding house in Southport. The curate died, suddenly, a few days after he had preached a sermon everybody talked about even after I was old enough to understand, tho' of course I wasn't even thought of at the time. "In my Father's house are many mansions", it began. "I go to prepare a place for you." And he did.

Dear pretty Aunt Jane. She lived with her school mistress sister, Martha, until she died in 1896, the year I was born, and later she kept house for Grandmother and her brood, and worked in the silk mill, (I still have some of the silk my mother bought in later years), and she it was who took my silent, fourteen-year-old mother, miserable and afraid, to work in the silk mill for money to pay for brother Ellis' music lessons. After three days of it, Aunt Jane said firmly, all four feet ten of her drawn up and deadly earnest, "I'm tekkin' her no more." That was all.

Another buddy of Grandmother's had a millinery establishment in the main thoroughfare (Bradshawgate it was, leading without looking right or left, from one end of the town to the other, into coal pits and workings and into fields and grim farmland at each end.) This lady (Miss Calland) was of a well-to-do, mill owning family, living in one of the three largest houses in the neighbourhood. She wanted to be an artist. She had all the promise in the world. I have one of her sketchbooks - streams that look like water, trees waving at you from the pages, hills you could really walk on - immediately recognisable for what they were. All done in the charcoal crayon usual in the 1860s. Her father played the Victorian father. "H'm. If she wants to draw, she can draw a needle!" And draw a needle she did; and hated men with a terrible, terrifying hatred.

In her workroom she taught my mother and one of her own nieces to make hats from nothing - a roll of wire and a few yards of ribbon, and perhaps a flower or two. One day a lady came and ordered a special hat which "must be in amber." Mother went to great trouble to get the right colour materials; but when the lady came to collect her hat she took one look and said, "That's not right! I ordered *amber*!" Mother protested that it was amber, whereupon the customer replied, "Oh! I allus thought amber were blue." So Mother began again to make a new hat, in blue.

And in the shop below the workroom, my mother met my father. He collected the money for the coal, supplied by the coal owner who'd taken my father to live with his family and work for them. (He was fourteen at that time and there was no one he belonged to anyway). He worked for that family all his life through, refusing jobs with both better pay and the appreciation they never gave him. But that is another story.

Miss Milliner must have approved of my father. She used to call upstairs when the bell tinkled and he came in, "Miss France! Shop, please!" And Mother had to come down the stairs and pay the coal bill, knowing full well, as she once told me, that Miss "Milliner" had done it on purpose.

They were both twenty when they became engaged and he gave her a silver locket. After a decorous Victorian interval they married. They were both twenty seven by then, but they'd had to work and earn and save, and she was taken as a bride to the little house he'd saved up for and had built for her within a mile or so's walking distance from the colliery, where he was a clerk and very soon secretary and general "maker-sure-that-everything worked-as-it-should," and "do-it-himself-if-it-didn't".

They were married at St. Mary the Virgin in Leigh, her family church, on December 10th 1890, and went to Blackpool for a brief honeymoon. Stepping out together along the Promenade, suddenly snow fell thick and fast and Will saw red blood streaming down his bride's face. She said, "It's all right Will, it's only the poppies in m' hat." And it was, under a crown of snow.

*"Bengal Street, Leigh, with St Mary the Virgin Parish Church. Slaughter house on the left."*

So the Recipe Book started. In my father's beautifully controlled readably clear handwriting. Black ink, nib dipped into a brass inkwell. I still have the inkwell. I think Gertrude must have dictated as Will wrote eg. *"Plum Pudding ... place over it a dusting of flour"* - my mother's usual "one cook to another" vague directions. She expected us to use common sense. Then there was *"a nut of butter"* - (no margarine in those early days). *"Cake"* ends in *"... bake in a moderate oven, not too quickly, lined with paper"*. I can see my father - the quiet humour of it in his eye as he couldn't quite share the joke, and couldn't help writing just what she said, to please her.

A revealing conglomeration of recipes. Food, furniture polish, cures, essentials like bread, and treacle toffee for fun - or was it health? Treacle toffee was good for coughs and sore throats - pleasanter far than gargling or the terrifying 'paint your throat' our doctor did to us.

Now come the first recipes (ingredients only), in Pal's writing, very clear. No "mode". I can hear him asking, "What next?" waiting to write, "how to make it". And my mother, a bit surprised, meeting the gentle, humorous eyes, "We've had 'mixing' before Will. Everybody will know what to do with those ingredients! It's always the same." And then, Will, *"I* wouldn't" and my mother-to-be, "Oh, well". After which the pen is dipped (or had he his beloved Waterman then? I wonder) and on we go to the only instruction to **raspberry sandwich**, as mother adds hurriedly, "Well, put "Bake twenty minutes" - and he does, smiling to himself, but kindly and with understanding of his beloved. No mention of raspberry jam. No wonder he was foxed.

### Raspberry Sandwich
*1 oz butter*
*1 egg*
*½ breakfast cup of sugar*
*1 cupful of flour*
*1 teaspoonful of cream of tartar*
*½ teaspoon carbonate of soda*

*Bake 20 minutes*

The second set of ingredients without "method" or "how to mix" is apparently **plain sponge cake** written in mother's flowing ever-generous hand. It has no heading. As often in this catalogue of ingredients, you are left to guess quantities: "A large cup of flour" (how large a cup?) a little milk, a little salt, the rind of a lemon (how large again?). Butter is specified, 2 oz, and baking powder (rather a lot, surely? say the 1980s) but no further guidance is given.

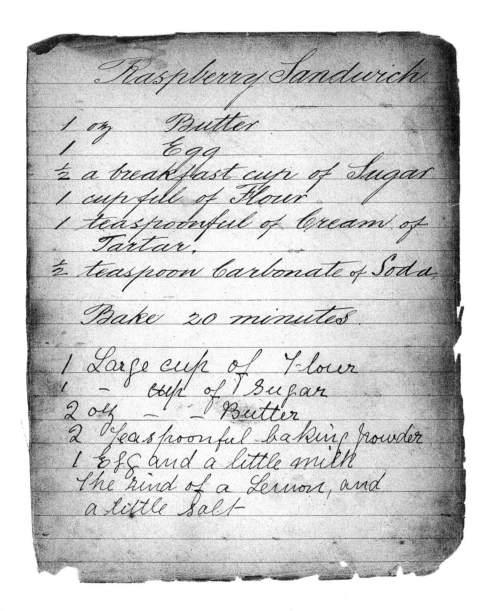

## Raspberry Sandwich

1 oz        Butter
1           Egg
½ a breakfast cup of Sugar
1 cupful of Flour
1 teaspoonful of Cream of
    Tartar.
½ teaspoon Carbonate of Soda,

Bake 20 minutes.

1 Large cup of Flour
1 - cup of Sugar
2 oz - - Butter
2 Teaspoonful baking powder
1 Egg and a little milk
The rind of a Lemon, and
    a little Salt

*Raspberry Sandwich, William Smith's handwriting above and Plain Sponge Cake, Gertrude Smith's handwriting below.*

### Plain Sponge Cake
*1 large cup of flour*
*1 cup of sugar*
*2 oz butter*
*2 teaspoonfuls baking powder*
*1 egg and a little milk*
*The rind of a lemon, and a little salt*

I'm afraid this recipe book is very higgledy-piggledy but it follows the course of time, and perforce we come to two domestic but inedible recipes in common use: **furniture paste** and **washing recipe**.

### Furniture Paste
*1oz beeswax,*
*1oz white wax,*
*1oz Castile soap*
*½ pint turpentine*
*½ pint water.*

*Dissolve beeswax and white wax in turpentine (warm). Dissolve Castile soap in the water (hot). Mix while warm and shake well.*

### Washing Recipe
*Slice 6 oz soap into a jar, adding 3 oz powdered borax, pour over both boiling water to fill the jar. Keep warm, and stir occasionally until thoroughly dissolved. This soap will keep any length of time. No soda is wanted nor is it necessary to boil the clothes.*

*Steep white clothes in cold water all night, with enough of this jelly added to give a froth on top of the clothes when they are well wetted. Next morning the borax will have drawn the dirt out so that only the merest trifle of rubbing is necessary. In winter the water may be warmer but in summer it is not necessary. The clothes can be rinsed and dried immediately. On the jelly water there must always be a froth; if it goes flat, more jelly is needed.*

*For flannels, put jelly into a pan, pour boiling water over it and then add cold water; work the woollens through the hands up and down until they feel soft and clean, but do not rub. Wring out, rinse and dry. If coloured things are left to soak in tepid water in which plenty of jelly has been dissolved, they will be half washed by the time the flannels are done. The jelly will wash silks, satins, feathers, laces, cottons or woollens beautifully.*

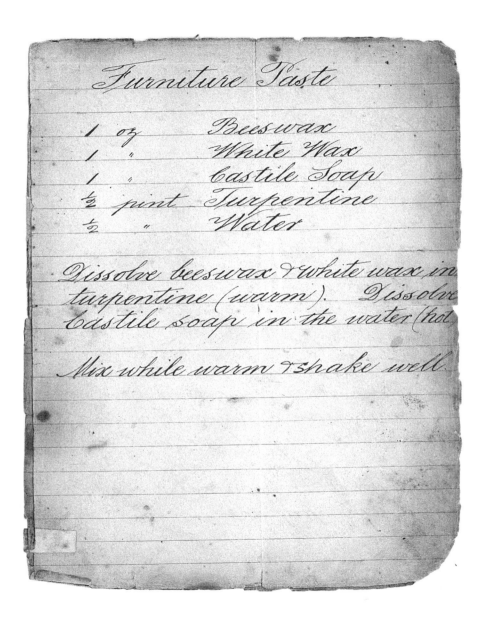

## Furniture Paste

| 1   | oz   | Beeswax     |
|-----|------|-------------|
| 1   | "    | White Wax   |
| 1   | "    | Castile Soap |
| ½   | pint | Turpentine  |
| ½   | "    | Water       |

Dissolve beeswax & white wax in turpentine (warm). Dissolve castile soap in the water (hot)

Mix while warm & shake well

*Furniture Paste, William Smith's handwriting.*

Tea-time may come in well enough here. My father, and others who joined him as the colliery business developed, came home for the then usual mid-day dinner of meat or fish and potatoes and other simple, well-known vegetables such as carrots, turnips, cabbage or cauliflower. No asparagus for us. I once heard my father say he did "like recognisable food". This came when he used to go every month to a sort of conference for the colliery owner who employed him from early boyhood. They were all otherwise heads of business firms concerned in some way with coal, like Pilkington's of St. Helens. Usually they lunched together at a well-known hotel in Liverpool. One day my father was disgusted to find a derelict carrot hidden among his mashed potatoes with his piece of grilled steak. Always after that, my mother provided a packet of sandwiches for his simple lunch, the "recognisable wholesome food" he preferred to hotel "questionables", however grand.

At the onset of winter there would probably be a huge tureen of hot *cockles and mussels* and a huge blue plate of brown bread and butter, around six p.m. for him and for us. Never was a meal eaten with more love, that I do know. So here comes the recipe; do not scorn it.

The cockles and mussels came fresh in the bag of the fisherman who gathered them by the sea that morning. They were what most of our neighbours could afford - a pint or more of each, boiled in a great iron can

*"Made by William Smith father of Gertrude (Bark). Pal's ship – 'Giddy Cauliflower' made c. 1885 – we (Bark family, Leamington) still have this."*

26

on the kitchen fire till they opened, then brought to the table in that dignified soup tureen dish in the same hot salty water. Mother served them, with a huge ladle, in bowls set before us, empty larger bowls along the middle of the table ready for the shells (fingers and forks, serviettes on knees, of course.) What more delectable than the brown and buttered bread on our side plate as we dug out succulent cockles and mussels, soaked in the sea. We were happy, sensibly and cheaply fed. We youngsters cleared the debris and washed up - it was quick. Cockleshells were saved. Our six foot by two foot garden would be decorated tomorrow. So might a homemade picture frame. Life was good, simple and of great interest. There were my father's tales too, ever absorbing, of great fun and freshness.

*The Bridgewater Canal at Bedford, Leigh from Mather Lane Bridge.*

Now for a winter dish - really good Lancashire **tripe and onions**- which approach with the reverence it deserves - of a vintage far removed from the leather hamburger just served for my ninety-two year old evening meal, bought in bulk (I've no doubt, as is the tomato) and tasting like linoleum! This nutritious dish, important through to old age, began as a pound or two of thick, fresh-bought tripe, usually fetched from the tripe shop, still warm, in a jug filled with a delicious liquor in which it had had its first boiling. Then we cut it into edible, fairly small pieces, (rejoicing to note the thick 'seams', where, in life, the tripe folded over); we added a generous amount of Spanish onions, chopped small, and cooked slowly in the same original liquor and with milk and a pinch or two of salt to taste. Simmer 'til all is tenderly edible. Remove from heat and thicken (we used to say 'lithe') with cornflour to make a good creamy sauce (no lumps except the tripe and onions - don't cook them away, only 'til tender for the most delicate or aged digestion). Serve, with dry toast or brown bread and butter, on soup plates (knives and forks) or bowls (dessert spoons). *This is a dish for an emperor, or a grandmother!*

Tripe is also good, so my father thought, if fried cold in dripping in a frying pan: very lightly, pale brown, not burnt or dried to the consistency of leather. Cut into edible pieces and fry gently in deep, real dripping (beef or bacon) quickly. Don't fry to black cinders!

These recipes date from my grandmother's days like many others, and lived good lives well into the 1980's, as I well know. Later, and even during the 1940 war, the tripe shop gave way to the unfortunate hamburger sort of ready food - and Chinese take-away (often swampy at best); and the white aproned, basket-bearing sea woman with bright sunshine smile under her freshly-ironed mutch was no more - cockles and mussels, like tripe, were rarely come by.

In spite of the style the next recipe is a most delicious ***lemon curd***. You need to add a little common sense in the mixing and the use of the jar! About this recipe, one little extra point. You will note that neither gas nor electricity has a place here. You stir until quite smooth over a slow fire. The discomfort cooks suffered in those days, glorious as our kitchen fire was in winter!

### Lemon Cheese
*2 lemons*
*½ lb sugar, finely powdered*
*3 oz butter*
*2 eggs*

*Grate off the yellow rind, and squeeze the juice out of the lemons. Put the eggs in last. Place the jar in a pan of hot water until hot through.*

And that reminds me - the Wax Doll. I must have been about five years old, having been awarded a small bentwood chair with a round decorated (with a wreath of flowers and nondescript leafage) - the perfection of possessions, and all for myself. I could easily carry it around from kitchen to parlour. Downstairs was alright. I was once caught on my ponderous way on the stairs, half way up, and realised how awful it felt to have so frightened my mother. The chair had gone clattering down; my mother thought otherwise and I didn't try that expedition again for a long time. My mother's kindly face was white.

But worse befell - for me. I had a doll, my first; she sat easily on the little bentwood chair, so one wintry day I put her there to warm by the kitchen fire. She did. But I looked again; she had no face. It was rolling down onto her frilly frock: horrible! I couldn't touch her - I looked and screamed in terror. Now, half a century - more like ninety years later - I know it was like a horror film of today. My mother, unfussy as ever, calmed the screams straight away. The horror is with me still, though I am long past 90.

Now with **pickled walnuts**, still my father's steady clerkly hand, we are translated over, perhaps, five years or so to our back yard, with Dickens, the bentwood chair, the stone window mullion - and along it trays of blackening walnuts, and a summer day. Why were those summer days always sunny and really warm and dependable? We girls had cotton dresses, for the summer: one red check, the other blue - a fashion gone and reviving (but not quite the same) more than once. Oh, those summer days - holidays and turning the walnuts in the sun. So easy to do for a child drowning in her father's beloved volumes of Dickens - sitting on the little bentwood chair in our sunny back yard, walled from the world, safe in a happiness of which we weren't aware until the first Great War shattered it less than ten years later.

### Pickled Walnuts
*Pick the walnuts, cover them overhead in strong salt and water, (about a handful of salt to a pint of water); cover over, and allow it to remain for 8 days.*

*Remove the cover and stir the walnuts every day. Drain off the water, and dry the walnuts on a cloth. Place them on a tray in the sun until they become black, turning them until they are black all over. Have ready some pickle jars, put the walnuts in those, with a little pickling spice. Boil the vinegar, and pour over the walnuts sufficient to cover them. Make the jars airtight and the walnuts will be ready for use in a month or two. Add 1½ oz of spice to every 100 walnuts, but if required extra hot, use 2 oz.*

The next recipe, **Pikelets**, are a winter rejoicing, and must be eaten as soon as cooked, piping hot, soused in butter and with a fork in hand. My mother used to have the mixture ready and all of us ready, herself at the cooker and frying pan (not too scorching hot - experience

*"William Smith in front of his office at John Speakman & Sons."*

## Pikelets

½ lb flour, ¼ pint milk.

¼ pint of water, 2 teaspoonfuls castor sugar 2, teaspoon baking powder ½ teaspoon salt, ¼ carbonate of soda & 1 egg. Put the flour in bowl & mix in gradually milk & water, drop in the yolk & mix to a smooth batter mix in a cup, the salt, sugar, & soda rubbing down all the lumps, add to the batter. Then add beaten up white & last of all add the baking powder. Have ready a warm well greased frying pan & put in about two table spoonfuls of batter. Fry until a golden brown turn & fry the other side.

My mother's recipe. Dawson She sent this to "The Clarion" When Julia asked for recipes. But the Editor said it was too 'good' for their readers — too expensive. These are most delicious pikelets, eaten as cooked with butter. 1998.

*The original hand written recipe for Pikelets.*

30

only will tell you how, even in these much later days of switches and degrees) at the ready. Consumers were ranged in an ever moving sort of queue (fairly in turn, and no dodging) plate and fork at the ready, butter pat and knife at hand near cook, who properly supervised as she cooked. 'Til mother called out, "No more left - sorry!", we ate our hot pikelets in heavenly content, and joined the end of the queue for our "Another, please!". There nearly always was, though I seem to hear my mother's twinkling, "How many have you had, love?" if she thought one of us had skipped a turn around the kitchen table. But it didn't often happen, though. If spotting somebody a little earlier than expected she would say, "I think somebody has skipped a place or two!" But they *were* good!

## Pikelets

*½ lb flour*
*¼ pint milk*
*¼ pint water*
*2 teaspoonfuls of caster sugar*
*2 teaspoonfuls of baking powder*
*½ teaspoonful salt*
*¼ teaspoonful carbonate of soda and one egg*

*Put the flour in a bowl and mix in gradually the milk and water. Drop in the yolk and mix to a smooth batter. Mix in a cup the salt, sugar and carbonate of soda, rubbing down all the lumps, and add to the batter. Then add beaten up white and last of all add the baking powder.*

*Have ready a warm, well greased frying pan and put in about 2 tablespoonfuls of batter, fry until a golden brown, turn and fry the other side.*

But pikelets were too expensive for Julia Dawson. Julia Dawson was the woman's editor of "The Clarion", the Socialist newspaper (sent afloat by Robert Blatchford and his friend and colleague, Thompson). This paper was taken week by week by my father. Julia Dawson put in a request for a recipe for pikelets for one of her do-it-yourself protégés. Mother, pen in hand, sent her recipe. She had a personal letter from Julia Dawson herself saying she had "tried her recipe herself and never met anything more delicious, but it was far too expensive as a commercial proposition".

These pikelets were delicious on a winter evening in our gas-lit kitchen after school or a bout of skating on Lion's Bridge Lake now sadly filled in and built upon. But then men would stand here and there around the lake holding a flaming torch. "Wheere's yon mon with cresset?" was a familiar question. "Owd John's gone for a pint. E's had enow of standing."

*Macaroni and Tomatoes, a new way with eggs, Dresden patties, salad dressing, lemon pudding* and another *haddock stuffed* follow. These are all in my pre-1914 handwriting and suggest visits to the houses of early friends at boarding school and profitable chats with their friendly cooks. All self-explanatory, all quite cheap and palatable. One, at least - fresh haddock stuffed - reminds me of my father's pleasure in "recognisable food" and simple ingredients; this recipe is highly recommended. Don't spoil it by serving vegetables. Offer brown homemade bread, buttered. The feeder will feel like a king and better, and cook's praise will ring indeed. (It is dated October 1909.)

### Fresh Haddock Stuffed

*A fresh haddock stuffed with sage and onions and baked in an oven. October 24 1909*

*Macaroni and Tomatoes* (Note: tomatoes are real tomatoes, not the highly seasoned semi-liquid tomatoes, people buy in tins in the 1980s, as they have for too long before. Use natural fruit, and make a dish worth the eating. It's worth the cook's trouble - peel the tomatoes.)

*Leigh's last coal mine, Bickershaw Colliery (also locally known as Plank Lane Colliery), Westleigh.*

### Macaroni and Tomatoes
*Place a layer of well boiled macaroni on a buttered tin with a little pepper and salt, then a layer of sliced peeled tomatoes. Next add a sprinkling of macaroni, cover with a white sauce onto which sift a little grated cheese, and also place a few small pieces of butter. Twenty mins in a quick oven to cook this nicely.*

**A new way with eggs.** After 1909, the English had taken to crossing the Channel now and then, and this recipe has a delicious variation - spinach instead of bread. I met this on a visit to a German friend in 1924. Now and then cook presents me with it in the nursing home. He takes the cover off with a flourish, "Eggs Florentine, eat it while it's 'ot!" I do. Like Bottom in "A Midsummer Night's Dream", I am translated.

### A new way of cooking eggs
*Take the required number of pieces of bread, butter them, and put on a very well buttered warm dish. Grate a sufficient quantity of cheese to thinly cover each piece, and carefully break an egg onto each slice, placing the whole in a hot oven just long enough for the eggs to set firmly, when it will be found the bread and cheese is quite ready also. Serve hot.*

**Dresden Patties** are evidence of topical taste in foreign (European) dishes. That satisfying Berlin pancake was a top favourite (soft and edible with plenty of good jam in the middle.) It changed its name to doughnut when the First World War began. American name but no improvement, I'm afraid, on the old Berlin pancake cookery.

### Dresden Patties
*Cut three slices of stale bread, about two inches thick; and stamp out rounds with a plain cutter, making them three inches in diameter. Hollow out the centre of each, leaving a case of bread. Cut a neat little round top to fit each case. Dip the cases for a few seconds in milk; then drain them. Chop finely half a pound of cold meat, one small onion, and a half a teaspoonful of parsley. Mix all these together, add a little gravy or sauce, and salt or pepper to taste. Brush cases of bread with beaten egg, cover with breadcrumbs, and fry golden brown. Make the meat mixture hot, fill cases with it, fry the lids and put them on, garnish the patties with fried parsley and serve hot.*

**Lemon pudding** marks a move to some modernity. The year (once again) is 1909, the writer (at grammar school still) is 13 years old, her writing far from distinguished. The gas oven is now "in" and is noted as "preferable" when the froth of lemon puddings top has to be "put in lumps on top" and baked till brown.

### Lemon Pudding

*Two large cupfuls of milk*
*Two large cupfuls of breadcrumbs*
*Three eggs (yolks only)*
*One teaspoonful of butter*
*One teaspoonful of lemon juice*
*One teacupful of granulated sugar*
*Rind of one lemon*
*One pinch of salt*

*Heat the milk and pour over the breadcrumbs. Allow to cool. Mix sugar, yolks of eggs, melted butter, salt, lemon juice and rind, well together, with crumbs. Butter a dish and put in. Bake in slow oven until quite set. Cover top with a layer of jam. Froth for top: Whites of eggs and castor sugar - beat well up into a froth. Put on pud in lumps and bake till browned slightly in a quick oven (gas stove oven preferable). October 21 1909 GS, 13 years*

### Miss Rabbit's recipes

The next recipes were written in 1910 when an Irish mother (black beaded dress and bonnet, indoors and out) and her schoolmistress daughter (young and sprightly) came to live in our street. Of course, my mother and they soon became friends. Miss Rabbit and her mother; I thought them very special. So they were. Miss Rabbit had holidays in Ireland, County Cork, "and we had rare fun too, all those young priests practising their job an' all." She sent me postcards with Irish stamps - one puzzled and rather annoyed me. "Friday", it began, "Keep your nose tidy". After all, I was at my Grammar School!

She taught school in Manchester - Ancoats, I think it was - and one Christmas she gave me a signet ring, just like hers, but with my initials blazoned on it. Her recipes were superb, so was her writing - even and round and merry like her jolly self.

She came round to our kitchen; and she and my mother made fudge together. Annie Rabbit liked to be called Renee- the name tripped so easily off the tongue! This is a simple and successful sweetmeat for beginners who might be put off by more complicated, longer flourishes.

Lemon Pudding.

Materials:—

Two large cupfuls of milk.
"        "        "        bread crumbs
Three eggs (yolks only)
One teaspoonful of butter.
"        "        "        lemon juice.
One teacupful of granulated sugar
Rind of one lemon.
Pinch of salt.

Hot the milk and pour over the bread crumbs
Allow to cool    Mix sugar, yolks of
eggs, melted butter, salt, lemon juice and
rind, well together, with crumbs.
Butter a dish and put in. Bake in slow oven
until quite set    Cover top with a layer
of jam.

Froth for Top.
whites of eggs and castor sugar ——— Beat well
up to a froth. Put on pud: in lumps and bake browned

*Lemon Pudding, GB's 13 year old handwriting.*

### Renee's Recipe
*2 lb gran. sugar*
*½ lb butter*
*Teacup of cold water*

*Put sugar and water in pan - dissolve - add butter - boil and test by dropping a little in cold water*

Try these recipes and certainly try **fudge** (though my mother made her fudge from a recipe culled from her special class in sweet making after 1923 when she came to visit me in Leamington Spa). This fudge is, however, a close second; and like my mother's, it wasn't chewy or hard, but melted in your mouth - superb! She made it for our home (Bedford in Leigh), and for Church bazaars and it sold more quickly than hot cakes. Sadly I can't include her recipe, though her Soft White Caramel (note 'soft') runs it pretty close. Try this. Note modern intrusion of 'nougat frame'. It suggests a tougher caramel rather than melting fudge.

*Mary (the maid) in later years with Annie Rabbit, Bill and EW (GB's sons) at Bond Street, Leigh.*

### Fudge
*lb sugar*
*1 large beaker of milk*
*Small oz of butter*
*Tablespoon glucose*
*Vanilla flavouring*
*3 oz plain fondant*
*Teacup of chopped nuts*

*Method: Sugar, milk, butter and glucose to dissolve in pan, boil to 238 degrees stirring occasionally. Allow to cool for 5 minutes, then add fondant which has been worked to a thin, pliable sheet with fingers - the vanilla essence and nuts -stir until it creams then pour into a nougat frame which has been lined with waxed paper. Allow to set then cut into bars , then cubes and wrap into waxed paper.*

### Soft White Caramel
*1¼ lbs sugar*
*2 oz of glucose*
*1 oz butter*
*Small half pint water*
*Teaspoon vanilla essence*

*Dissolve sugar, glucose and water, boil to 230 degrees. Add the butter and vanilla essence and boil to 236 degrees. Then pour into a bowl which has been rinsed out in cold water, leave until half cool. Beat into a cream, leave to stand for 20 minutes, covered with waxed paper. Put in pan, place in one containing half pint of boiling water, melt, add a few drops of lukewarm water, and warm until it will just pour. Pour into a nougat frame covered with waxed paper, and leave to set. Cut into cubes placed far apart and leave for some hours to dry. Then they may be packed in a box to keep them from the air.*

**Exeter Stew** *and* **Savoury Balls** (in my teen-age pencil): real beef, only ½ lb, an onion, only 1 oz butter and 1 oz flour with a carrot and, "a little herbaceous mixture." Details of procedure proclaim the economy and also the tasty flavour of this quite substantial dinner for four good trencher men and women. You'll agree if you follow the recipe carefully and don't frizzle the butter away.

### Exeter Stew
*½ lb beef*
*1 onion*
*¾ pint water*
*1 oz butter*
*1 oz flour*
*A little herbaceous mixture*
*Pepper and salt to taste*

*Heat the butter in a saucepan and brown the sliced onion; add the flour and mix well; add the water by degrees, boil up, then add the meat, cut into squares the sliced carrot, pepper and salt, simmer slowly 1 ½ hours.*

*Savoury Balls* gives you ingredients. Roll mixture into balls the size of a walnut, and note that parsley (fresh, please) and suet (real not packet then, though you may use it now and with advantage.)

Do try this superlative meal on a wintry day. Note time for cooking meat section; and adding balls for ¾ hour extra cooking.

### Savoury Balls
*¼ lb flour*
*2 oz minced suet*
*½ teaspoonful minced parsley*
*Teaspoon salt*
*A little less than ½ teaspoonful pepper*
*A little herbaceous mixture*
*¼ teaspoon baking powder*

*Mode - Put flour on a board, shred and chop the suet finely with it. Add all ingredients and mix to a stiff paste with a little water, form into balls size walnut and drop into the stew, cook ¾ hour.*

### Miss Yates' Recipes

My mother made our dresses herself, at the same Victorian Singer machine (in the kitchen) which now lives with and works perfectly for- no trouble she says - one of my daughters-in-law. Our special dresses and coats were made by Miss Yates and her sister dressmaker, a terribly fusty experience and penance for a teenager who lived with fresh air and open windows and had just embarked upon her co-ed Grammar School (2 good miles walk there and back, 'til I was overwhelmed by a secondhand bicycle on turning 15). This was 1910 or 1911.

I hated "trying on" at Miss Yates's. I think it was the most unfresh place ever invented. I couldn't believe that my mother didn't seem as sick in that smelly atmosphere as I felt. But she was always pleasant and calm, talking recipes with one Miss Yates while the other put pins into me and knelt on the carpet to fix the length. I had to twirl round while she did it and the sickening smell of Miss Yates washed round with her.

It was a lovely dress, though: "peacock blue velvet" (they kept saying, in sort of respectful voices). And it was special, my first for my first grammar school Christmas dance. I nearly died with pride, it was so lovely in spite of Miss Yates's smells. And I was escorted home after the dance,

*Jones's Buildings (where William Smith was born) and the shop next door.*

by a hitherto unknown, quite tall "old boy" who was at Oxford. I did not like him at all, and I said, firmly, "You can go back now - this is my father coming to meet me. I'm alright now, thank you!" My beloved father (known to me as "Pal" always) thanked him "for taking care of my daughter". All the stars sang in heaven as I took my father's offered arm. (So much for Oxford).

Anyhow Miss Yates (each of them) was a good dressmaker, though her smell never became bearable. She once made me a thick winter coat, blue again; and the buttons had a pattern on them, like silver, of a lady with long wavy hair and the word "FLU" on them. I still have one as a brooch, but I've no idea what it means, if anything.

It's a useful recipe too, Miss Yates' Queen Cake - worth trying. I'm sorry I didn't take more kindly to the two Miss Yates. They both had terribly disappointing, long, pasty faces. I realise now that life couldn't have been hilariously pleasant for them making clothes for ungrateful little girls all the time; except for my mother of course. Talking recipes with her, swapping recipes with her, may have made a brightness, even a sweetness in that awful stuffy room.

### Miss Yates' Queen Cakes
*½ lb flour*
*¼ lb butter*
*¼ lb granulated sugar*
*4 teaspoonsful of baking powder*
*2 eggs and a little milk if required*
*Raisins or currants and candied peel according to taste or liking, equally nice any way.*

*Butter first, and then sugar then eggs, flour and baking powder together then dry fruit. Bake in a slow oven until brown. Work the butter to a cream; dredge in the flour, add the sugar and currants and mix all well together; whisk the eggs, mix them with the cream and flavouring and stir these into the flour, beat the paste well for 10 minutes, add the baking powder, put it into small buttered pans, and bake the cakes from ¼ to ½ hour.*

**Coconut Biscuits** (another Miss Yates dressmaker recipe) are straightforward. A greased tin is a pleasant homely instruction - especially if a twelve or thirteen year old child is watching. My mother's eye for colour comes characteristically into the last sentence: *"They should be a pale straw colour".*

### Miss Yates' Coconut Biscuits
*½ desiccated coconut*
*4 oz caster sugar*
*3 eggs*
*1 ½ oz cornflour*

*Mix together dry ingredients. Whisk to a very stiff froth the whites of eggs, add gradually some to the dry ingredients using only just enough white to bind the mixture together. It should not crumble when a little is pressed together, if too much white is used the cake will run flat instead of standing up in high heaps. Lay a sheet of paper on a tin, and place the mixture into small high heaps as rough as possible. Bake first in rather hot oven for 5 minutes to set the egg and prevent it spreading, then in slow oven about half an hour or until they are crisp. They should be a pale straw colour when done.*

**Miss Yates' Welsh Cheese Tarts** The instructions explain clearly enough why we always called these "upside down cakes".

### Miss Yates' Welsh Cheese Tarts
*Weight in butter, sugar and flour of an egg. ¼ teaspoonful of baking powder, grated rind of a lemon also a little lemon juice. Beat the butter and sugar together add half the egg and flour. Mix well, then the other half, together with baking powder and lemon. Line some tins with paste, spread a little jam at the bottom, cover mixture, bake until brown.*

Now follows a little frivolity (pre First World War in 1914). **Puff Pastry** in my mother's interested, absorbed, hurried writing (there were so many calls on her, so little wasted time, ever); all very clear, both ingredients and method. Puff pastry made light with the juice of one lemon. They were honest, big enough lemons in those pre-1914 war days.

### Puff Pastry
*1 ½ lb flour to 1 lb lard*

*Mix flour with all the lard in flakes. In remaining flour mix juice of one lemon, pinch of salt and water to make a nice paste, roll out and put on flakes, turn over and place another layer, repeat until finished, then roll out again.*

**Marzipan potatoes** are extra frivolous. Quick and easy for a 12 year old to make; much more quickly and readily eaten.

### Marzipan potatoes
*¼ lb ground almonds*
*½ lb caster sugar*
*1 egg*

*Mix all well together and roll in cocoa or chocolate powder.*

Next **Sponge Roll** and **Fruit Cake** - brevity and straightforward, chatty style - note "not quite" ¼ lb granulated sugar; peel and sultanas "just as much as you like" - the tolerance and expectation of cook's taste!!

### Sponge Roll
*1 cup flour (large)*
*1 cup sugar, 2 eggs*
*2 teaspoonsful of baking powder*

*Bake for a few minutes until a nice brown; roll over then spread with jam.*

**Fruit Cake**
¼ *lb butter, or half lard*
¼ *lb flour*
¼ *lb sugar (not quite)*
*1 teaspoonful baking powder*
*2oz rice flour,*
*1 dessert spoon of golden syrup*
*1 egg and a little milk*
*Candied peel and sultanas, just as much as you like*

*Add syrup after creaming butter and sugar. Mix two flours and baking powder together.*

**Ginger Wine** Grandmother France, (my mother's mother) made this long before 1910; but it dates from a family summer holiday in Southport - the seaside where the sea was always receding and washing ashore further and further out. Grandmother always kept a bottle in the sideboard in her bedroom. When she became very old - and independent, refusing to live with any of her family, though up to the end she visited them - her family persuaded her to have Miss Wilkinson look after her in her own little old cottage. There was no bathroom, just a tub in front of the kitchen fire. My mother and I went round to say "good night", but no one answered the door, so we called to Grandmother through the window and heard "I don't want Miss Wilkinson anymore. I'm all right. I'll see you tomorrow. Good night". We had to be satisfied. Lancashire independence.

A few short years and I was married. I went home for a few days and went round with Mother to say good night to Grandmother. This time we had a key. She was 85, still charming and pretty and pleasant, and enjoying a sip of her homemade Ginger Wine - an abstemious family to the last. Sitting forward in her bed, Grandmother nodded to me and said, "I'm so glad you've come. Fetch me a little of my ginger wine. It's in the cupboard where it always was. Don't bother to put it in a glass. Just moisten my lips". I did just that. She didn't live many hours after!

**Ginger Wine**
*3 drams tincture of ginger*
*3 drams Capsicum*
*1d worth essence of lemon (mixture)*
*2 lbs granulated sugar*
*¾ oz tartaric acid*
*6 gills boiling water*
*6 gills cold water*

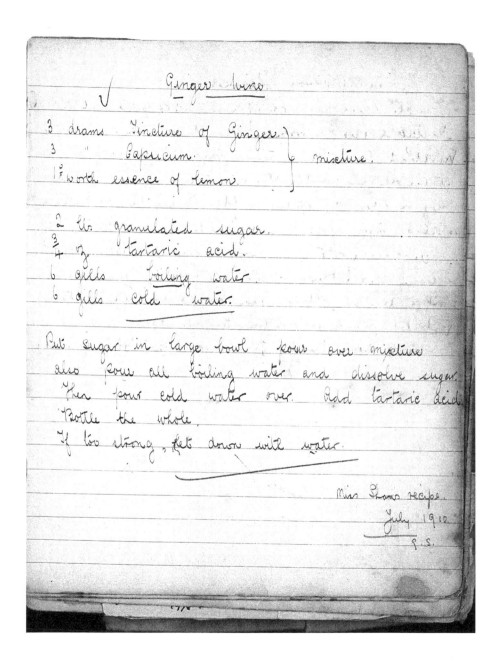

Ginger Wine.

✓

3 drams   Tincture of Ginger. ⎞
3    "       Capsicum.          ⎬ mixture.
1½ worth essence of lemon.      ⎠

2 lb. granulated sugar.
¾ oz. tartaric acid.
6 gills boiling water
6 gills cold water.

Put sugar in large bowl, pour over mixture
also pour all boiling water and dissolve sugar.
Then pour cold water over. Add tartaric acid.
Bottle the whole.
If too strong, let down with water.

Miss Shaw recipe.
July 1910
P.S.

*Ginger Wine, Miss Shaw's recipe, July 1910.*

43

**Ginger Wine (contin.)**
*Put sugar in large bowl, pour over mixture also pour all boiling water and dissolve sugar. Then pour cold water over. Add tartaric acid. Bottle the whole. If too strong, let down with water. Miss Shaw's recipe, July 1910*

**Turkish Delight (Alice's Recipe) and The Elms** Turkish Delight belongs to about 1910 too, and my earliest school friend's home, "The Elms", in the country about three miles from my home, with Alice the maid, in Broderie Anglaise cap and apron, spick and span.

**Turkish Delight (Alice's Recipe)**
*Soak a 1 ¼ oz packet of gelatine overnight in a teacupful of water (cold). Put a pound and a half of loaf sugar in an enamelled saucepan, with a small teacupful of water. Let it stand until the sugar is dissolved, then add the gelatine, the juice of two lemons and one teaspoonful of essence of lemon. Stir till it boils; boil nine minutes. Rinse two dishes in cold water, pour the mixture into each, and colour one with cochineal. Let it stand overnight, cut into squares, and roll in icing sugar.*

Alice's recipe explains itself. If you like this kind of stick-jaw stuff, do try it - or make little Christmas parcels of it, with Miss Rabbit's splendid fudge for your friends. A sure winner.

It was the period of the "Merry Widow" curls - my friend (from "The Elms") and I tried to make them on visits to one another's homes. It was the time of rather superior doll's clothing and we did rather vie over this; and feelings (jealousy?) rampaged a bit. I don't remember that our friendship suffered at all: our little circle of two far away, highly-placed Boarding Schoolers, one already at home, education over; and local 16th century established grammar school for me.

My grammar school was co-ed, as they say nowadays, and within walking distance through a busy grimy town. I lost my infant faith in prayer over going to this school. For nights and days before I joined its ranks, I prayed in simple belief that it would burn down before I went. It didn't. And as autumn closed round me, in I went, and lost myself along a maze of murmuring corridors - up resounding, endless staircases and down.

I had been allotted to Form 4A, so I knocked and fearfully entered what was marked 4A. Surprise, surprise. Brusquely, "You're 5K," barked at me from a tousle headed woman wearing an academic gown (I didn't know what it was then). "Oh no," I met her kindly eyes, "I'm not good enough for that - too high." Howls from the assembled tormentors. Here was, they saw

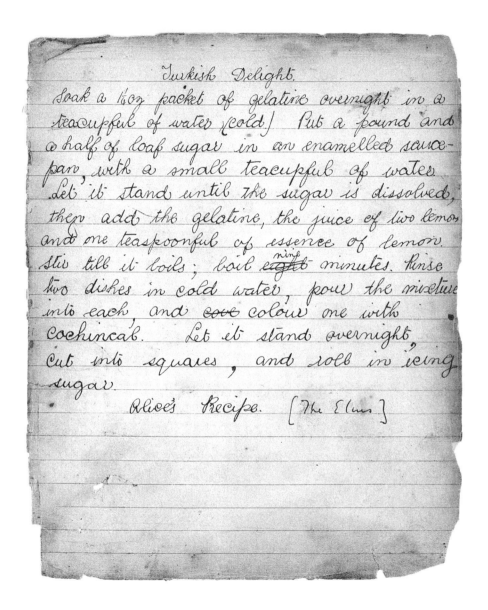

Turkish Delight.

Soak a ½oz packet of gelatine overnight in a teacupful of water (cold.) Put a pound and a half of loaf sugar in an enamelled saucepan, with a small teacupful of water. Let it stand until the sugar is dissolved; then add the gelatine, the juice of two lemons and one teaspoonful of essence of lemon. Stir till it boils; boil nine minutes. Rinse two dishes in cold water, pour the mixture into each, and colour one with cochineal. Let it stand overnight. Cut into squares, and roll in icing sugar.

Alice's Recipe. [The Elms]

*Turkish Delight, Alice's Recipe.*

with glee, a fool indeed. But Miss Marshall as she turned out to be, swung round on them, said not a word. Silence; then to me, "We're upside down in this school; I'm afraid you're in 4C - it's my form anyway. See you next lesson; I'm Geography". I stumbled out, she followed and led me to my rightful, lowly room. Wonder of wonders! A youngish man was holding forth, his face aglow, the class entranced, about Charles Dickens and "Great Expectations". We smiled at one another across the room, Miss Marshall exchanged a word or two with him, and went. I took the empty desk. Dickens!? This was all right; I was at home again in the summer sunshine of our glorious back yard. And I loved Miss Marshall.

Four years or so later, the young teacher of English (also revered) went to War and was killed. His wife (also a beloved teacher) gave me a book of his in remembrance: Hazlitt's Essays, for I was off to University and an English degree like theirs, and holiday teaching at the old school in a few years. Life became more than I could nonchalantly cope with far too soon.

Back to "The Elms" for a minute. The mother played superbly - on an Ibach grand piano. Sometimes I stayed overnight, and she egged me on to play duets with her. Her daughter, my friend, was home from her Boarding School as was customary with such families' young ladies. We were friends all our lives after "Dame School".

Monday at "The Elms" was washing-day. A washerwoman took possession of an outbuilding roaring with the laundry equipment of 1910: boiler for water, stoked beneath with coal, tubs galore. Drying happened on lines spread along adjacent paths along the back of the house; and we (the women and girls of the house) were in the kitchen, wielding five heated irons encased in metal slippers and constantly reheated at the roaring coal fire, rubbing and folding like mad as one of us brought in a basket full of sweet-smelling laundry from the line. The mother sat coy on a Windsor chair and encouraged our labour. My friend's father strolled in, diamond ring sparkling (a man wearing jewellery? I thought. My father never would - real men didn't). But, tho' as at table, no one spoke a word until Father did, I burst out when he cracked a joke over our "playing at ironing". "How many handkerchiefs?" when I offered him an iron - "see whether you can race me!" He grinned and bubbled and even the rest of the family giggled a bit. Then came dinner - 1 o'clock, ceremony and silence. (At breakfast, the cracking of the eggs on Sunday was like rifle practice!)

There was the garden. Father G took me round to admire his roses. That was easy - they were lovelier than I'd ever dreamt possible and Father G carefully cut me a celestial, overflowing bunch to take home, "for my mother". I, gratefully - "Oh, thank you!" I walked in fairyland then. Now, I think he was glad to have pleased and surprised his quiet daughter's young friend who chattered to him and seemed happy and at home in his company. For me, fathers were all for loving and happy talk, I thought. And here was a father. So we talked.

Alice used to wear plain uniform till after mid-day dinner - cap and speckled apron: after that, it was that pretty white embroidery cap with two flowing streamers down her hardworking back. A comfortable presence, Alice. And my roses for my mother and home. Our two yard wide coal-dust front garden patch at home sprouted only a privet border along the street and round the corner, and a gorgeous pink rhododendron bush - our "rosydandrums" was what the passing coal-miners called it, and so did we children - a splendid word, it had a fragrance about it.

## Cousin Dick's recipes

In early days at Grammar School, the Maths master lost his temper over my stupidity and said I "just sat there like a pot mule". I hadn't been prepared for that (even at 14) and just looked him in the eye, and sat. I thought him very rude though. He was young and dashing and married to a local

*"Cousin Dick outside the workhouse at Leigh where my uncle and aunt were Workhouse Master and Matron."*

Headmaster's (not ours) daughter. It wasn't long before he departed to another school; but not 'til after his encounter with my skilful cousin - Dick France, a special cousin of mine, just a few months younger than I. He had red hair and feared nothing.

Of course, I'd told my cousin about "pot mule" - not pleasing to hear, probably but not without cause, I admit. I never mastered algebra or found out why x=o could possibly make life jolly or useful - not like poetry. I met that at the same school and loved it all my life, and Dickens, because my father had a bookcase full of him, and even Shakespeare. Soon afterwards, this rude master was insulting to some girl in my cousin's form, and redhead Dick leapt onto the dais, seized him by his posh necktie and nearly strangled him before they could be

*Richard France (Cousin Dick) in 1914, just before he went to the War.*

parted. The class cheered, I was told afterwards; and Dick said it had been "worth it" - the "six of the best" the Headmaster gave him. "Not your best behaviour, France, I'm sorry but..." and France, quite kindly accepting the - was it apology in the Headmaster's eye? - "It's alright, sir".

Years later the new Headmaster told me this. He was the German Master, much beloved, at the time; and the staff room had rocked with the tale. Then when the 1914 War began, France called at the school to bid the Headmaster farewell. The same Headmaster recalled how my cousin saluted him with "Good bye Sir", turned, saw the cane and saluted it! "Good bye old friend!" and went. He was 19. He went straight to the Somme and he never came back.

His recipe for ***treacle toffee*** and my own for the ***chocolate cake*** both he (and my own sons later) much approved of. They fit very well at this point perhaps. We made it with blithe spirit, before that 1914 War that took him forever; brightness fell from the air and remained - cheery, bright spirit.

**Black Treacle Toffee** - *Dick's Recipe (Pre- 1916)*
*6 oz sugar*
*2 oz butter*
*2 teaspoonfuls syrup*
*½ cup of Nestles Milk*

**Chocolate Cake**
*¼ lb butter*
*¼ lb sugar*

*Beat to a cream. Add 1 beaten egg. Add 2 tablespoonfuls chocolate powder to ½ lb flour and mix; then add and mix well with the rest. A little milk, if necessary. A little vanilla essence. (I didn't put any essence in.) This is Dick's favourite.*

This chocolate cake is evidently worth making, as Dick had considered the possibility of his being wounded and arriving during some starshine night in Manchester "all the way from the trenches" he said - "and be sure to have a chunk of your chocolate cake in your pocket for me." 1916 had broken on us then. I was an unimportant Red Cross Nurse, in the University Detachment on duty o' nights, sorting out as best we could train loads of wounded on their way to neighbouring Lancashire hospitals, providing tea (they were ready for it), and sometimes joining their painful, thankful ambulance jolt "doing what we could to help". But that is quite another story.

### Miss Mosscrop's Recipes

And on to **Icing for cakes** and **cream buns** - almost a whole, very detailed page of Will's neat, smaller sized writing, winding up with "Miss Mosscrop's Recipe" after a reference to whipped cream which is not an obligatory item, evidently.

*Lanford Hall Hospital, 1916, GB second from the left.*

Miss Mosscrop, who took the cookery classes, was my young idea of a spinster. She was a learned cookery teacher who wore a large floppy hat (both indoors and out) with hat pins that wobbled as she walked with short, non-committal firm steps. She was probably only about 40, but exuded an aura of tremendous antiquity which we young folks thought wildly funny.

Miss Mosscrop was a great friend of Matilda Smith (also a teacher) who was a France family friend. (Two of my aunts-in-law were school ma'ams as my grandmother's sister had been years before until 1896).

### Icing for Cakes
*½ breakfast cup of pulverised sugar*
*A few drops of cold water*
*A few drops of essence of lemon*

### Cream Buns
*¼ pint of water: 1 egg: 1 oz sifted flour: 1 oz butter. Put water and butter in pan, bring to the boil, add the sifted flour. Stir until quite smooth over slow fire. Turn out to cool, then add egg well beaten. Beat the mixture 10 mins. Place dessert spoonful of this mixture on slightly greased baking tins. Bake in moderate oven until nice brown and set aside. When cold fill with whipped cream, sweetened and flavoured if liked.*
*(Miss Mosscrop's Recipe)*

Cream buns comes of my mother's attending municipal cookery classes. She was a frequent pursuer of such knowledge, during two Great Wars, and in between them. Even in her late sixties, visiting me (and later, living in Leamington with me) mother joined Mr. Wood's sweet-making classes. Her caramels sold like wild fire at church bazaars, and mother's beautifully wrapped (by my father, of course) sweets were in constant demand for many years. She made no more after my father died, in 1940, and we were plunged into war again.

Cream buns were not at all a usual occurrence in my home, 36 Guest Street, Leigh. I don't remember their ever happening, but there does seem to be a touch of style about my father's adding, "Miss Mosscrop's Recipes". The recipe for Miss Mosscrop's cream buns is sprinkled with what I think must be my father's meticulously extracted information dealt out by his beloved, and here and there paraphrased by him. For example, when the mixing is done you *"place a dessert spoonful of this mixture on slightly greased baking tins"*. These baking tins - three sizes - were still in use when I was in my eighties; and a proud woman was I to have them in the drawer of the kitchen dresser that my father made. I had known it all my life.

We had little furniture he had not made: stools of many sizes and shapes, and a writing desk (the backs bearing the name of the products they contained as a box); my "dressing table" when I was old enough to need one with three drawers; bookshelves, of which there were three vintages, according to the books I acquired as I grew older through childhood, schools, college. All made of odd wood and great, loving care. I've loved these all my life and love them still. These many objects were still part of my Leamington home when it was dismantled in 1985.

Miss Mosscrop must have impressed my early years quite noticeably; for I remember her remark to her friend (known as Aunt Till) when she was terrifyingly distraught over some scandalous comment on herself; "Someone has *maligned* you Till!" I pondered long over what horror hid in that word, imagining worse horrors to befall our kind little "Aunt Tilly" until of course, I asked my father and I added a useful word to my eight year old vocabulary. The spelling was beyond me, but the sound rang splendidly.

Next I like the "please yourself" atmosphere of Auntie Tilly's **beef and ham roll** but am rather discouraged by the lavish quantities of beef and ham. You may not be now so don't be repelled. There's only one egg required. You may boil it in a cloth or in a jar or mould *if preferred* .

### Aunt Tilly's Beef and Ham Roll
*1 lb lean beef*
*1 lb ham or bacon*
*1 egg*
*4 to 6 oz bread crumbs*
*dried parsley and salt and pepper to taste*

*Mince beef and ham, add bread crumbs and herbs and last of all the egg. Roll out on a floured baking board and boil in a cloth for 2 hours or in a jar or mould if preferred.*

One more pudding, not to be missed - the recipe tells you all you need to know; go ahead!

### Ginger Sponge Pudding
*¼ lb flour*
*3 tablespoons syrup*
*One egg, 2 oz suet*
*½ teaspoon bicarbonate of soda*
*3 tablespoons milk*
*One teaspoon ground ginger*

*"The track that ran between the canal wharf and the colliery."*

### Ginger Sponge Pudding (contin.)

*Chop suet and mix all dry ingredients together (underlined). Mix thoroughly with syrup, egg and milk and pour into well-buttered mould. Steam 1½ hours. Turn onto hot dish and serve with custard or white sauce.*

Now come two bread pudding recipes, evidently less offensive than the dry chunks - pockmarked with currants- which I get now (aged 92 in a "nursing home").

***Yately and Chocolate Bread Puddings*** in my early teenage grammar school pencil writing and underwritten "Gert's Recipe". Maybe, my school had drafted a few girls, including me, into cookery class then in despair at my prowess in science. My Fifth Form heavily applauded my 4% for Chemistry the previous Xmas exam. But they pumped up my second-hand bicycle for me, all the same. We weren't bad friends, we shared our jokes, and they knew I was pleased with my 4%. I preferred English. (Mr. Clarke and his jolly, ramshackle family home were seeing to that then; and "dear old Oliver" taught German poetry.)

### Yately Bread Pudding
*Boil a small piece of thin lemon peel in three parts of a pint of milk, add two tablespoonfuls of sugar, then pour over two rounds of stale bread. Let it stand for ten minutes. Grease a pudding dish with butter, and put a thin layer of lemon cheese in the bottom.*

*Then beat the bread and milk up thoroughly, taking out all the lumps and pour it gently over the lemon cheese. Lastly beat up an egg with the remainder of the pint of milk, and pour over the whole. Bake in a moderate oven for about a half hour or until set.*

### Chocolate Bread Pudding
*Soak two cupfuls stale breadcrumbs in four cupfuls scalded milk for a half hour. Melt two squares chocolate in a saucepan placed over boiling water. When melted add ⅓ cupful of sugar and enough milk to make it of a consistency to pour. Mix sugar, breadcrumbs, milk and chocolate, then add ¼ teaspoonful salt, and half a cupful of blanched and shredded almonds, twelve drops of vanilla, and two eggs well beaten. Put mixture into a greased pudding dish and bake for one hour in a moderate oven.*

*If desired, the yolks only of eggs may be beaten in, the whites being used to make a meringue on the top of the pudding.*

*Cost = milk, one penny, eggs, two pennies, chocolate two pence, sugar, almonds etc = one penny. Total six pennies, enough for six persons.*
*(Gert's recipe)*

Note the price list at the end of chocolate bread pudding. We dealt in pennies in those days - worth much more than they are today in 1988.

Now, **to cook fish tastily**. It's hard to believe that we could afford two pounds of haddock or whiting nowadays (1988). Pre-1914, when fish and chip shops abounded and fishermen went out from Fleetwood, good fish was less costly to buy - eels (cooked as in Shakespeare's day - remember Anne of Cleves and Henry VIII? - were delicious. Where are they now?) and herring and plaice, large and small. A straightforward recipe (note "parboiled") but go gently with salt, and be fairly lavish with finely chopped fresh parsley. And use haddock rather than whiting (many small bones) though whiting has the more delicate flavour. Do not use salted haddock, please. So then the recipe:

### To cook fish tastily

*Take two pounds of filleted haddock or whiting. Parboil and drip the water off, then place flat in a well-buttered tin, covering the fish with a thin white sauce; sprinkle pepper and salt to taste. Cover again with a layer of well-buttered crumbs; over this spread finely shredded parsley and squeeze a little lemon juice. Place in a hot oven and bake for twenty minutes.*

***Kidney Soup** and **Invalid Custard**.* My mother's writing ran together these two evidently strengthening "getting better from an illness" dishes. Note *"simmer gently two hours"*. This suggests the use of a gas cooker, more readily controllable than an open fire, for simmering and producing good nourishment. This was a penance, it really was a misery. I could read Dickens with one arm while stirring for about an hour during which my other arm gradually became parboiled - most uncomfortable.

### Kidney Soup

*1 lb ox kidney*
*1 onion*
*1 small carrot*
*1 small turnip*
*1 ½ pints water*
*2 cloves*
*1 ½ oz flour and 2 oz butter or dripping*

*Cut kidney and wash removing all white bits inside, toss the kidney in flour, melt butter in pan and brown kidney in pan over smooth fire, then add water, stir until boiling, clean the vegetables, add the onions with cloves inside, P and S, simmer gently for two hours. Strain and serve with pieces if liked.*

### Invalid Custard

*One egg*
*Sugar to taste*
*Half pint milk*

*Beat egg, add sugar to taste, set in a pan of cold water, and allow to stand in hot water about one hour.*

The 1914-18 war seems to be simmering too, after my mother's kidney soup and invalid custard. There are a few recipes like ***casserole potatoes*** which I don't remember meeting - unlike ***lemon cheese*** which was an ever welcome addition to the five o'clock tea with brown homemade bread. Note: never buttered and so losing the lemony sharpness and the wonder and goodness of the brown bread.

There now appear names of friends and neighbours among more exotic recipes my mother hurriedly wrote when she began to attend Miss Mosscrop's (of the wobbly hats) cookery classes. She and my mother were cookery minded and these classes swelled with the war. Other ladies' names, e.g. Pennington and Miss Wilson were evidently of Miss Mosscrop's 1912 onward cookery class. Not Miss Grounds (a superb fruit jam) who was the vicar's housekeeper, a friend of my mother and me, among other young things, the gentle, firm vicar's "guardian".

*"The milkman with his cart on his rounds in Leigh"*.

### Miss Wilson's Edinburgh Parkin
*One pound flour, half butter, half brown sugar, one teaspoon ground ginger, half carbonate soda, half cream tartar. Bake 15 to 20 minutes after pressing well into a flat tin. Cut into pieces.*

(Note *"pressing well into a flat tin."* Good old Scottish Miss Wilson!)

### Raspberry Buns
*Half flour*
*2 oz butter*
*2 oz lard*
*2 oz ground rice*
*2 oz caster sugar*
*2 eggs*
*Good half teaspoon of baking powder*
*2 tablespoons of milk or more.*

### Raspberry Buns (contin.)
*Put flour and shortening on board. Put all dry ingredients in a bowl. Beat up eggs, keep back little to brush over. Add eggs and milk to dry ingredients. Divide in nine pieces, make a hole on top of each piece and put in jam. Cover over. Bake in oven 20 minutes. Brush over with the egg.*

You must follow these briefly lucid instructions meticulously, even into covering the hole you've made in the joyfully delicious bun. Note the even mixture of butter and lard. This results in neither cake nor pastry. Bite and you taste food for the gods - ambrosial.

***Caramel Toffee.*** Mother's toffee, easy to make and enjoy. Try this. Note the arrival of Glucose, beginning to be favoured in ladies' toffee making from now on.

### Caramel Toffee
*One lb sugar, ¼ lb sugar, ¼ lb butter, thereupon tin Swiss milk, juice ¼ lemon, 2 tablespoonful Glucose, cup of water.*

Another ***Parkin*** with a few introductions to make it a bit different from others. Worth trying because of the dripping. (You should always fry bread in dripping and serve with a lightly poached egg. Do not burn or harden the

*Back street between houses on Garden Street and Glebe Street, looking towards Leigh Parish Church from Kirkhall Lane, Westleigh.*

celestial dripping toast - gently does it - a dish for someone who has lost all interest in food. Tempting.)

### Parkin
*1½ lb oatmeal*
*½ lb flour*
*¼ butter*
*¼ dripping*
*¼ sugar*
*2 lbs syrup*
*1 oz ginger*
*½ gill milk*
*Teaspoon of soda*

*Bake one hour slow oven.*

**Leicester cake** - needs a concentrating cook, a rare commodity in these days, but it's a good, solid keeping cake and the almond paste adds the touch of extra glory. Hungry males take to it, so persevere - and remember - clean the currants - they can be unexpectedly and grittily unpleasant to the palate.

### Leicester cake
*½ lb flour*
*2 oz lard*
*2 oz butter*
*¼ lb currants*
*¼ sultanas*
*¼ mixed fruit*
*¼ raw sugar*
*2 eggs or three if preferred*
*¼ teaspoon carbonate soda*
*2 oz almonds, 2 teaspoons syrup*
*A few mixed spices steeped in wine*
*Milk to mix*

*Clean currants and fruit and cut peel quite small, beat the eggs, rub the shortening in flour, add dry ingredients except soda, mix well, a tiny pinch of salt, add the eggs and treacle, spice to cover a threepenny piece. Add to eggs, the carbonate soda must be mixed with a little milk and added the last thing. Bake in a slow oven about two hours.*

***Welsh Rarebit.*** One expects everyone to make this by nature, but the final dishing of this recipe is what makes it. Instructions are clear and worth following. It was a much welcome dish of my mother's - always enjoyed, especially in winter weather. So, nota bene.

### Welsh Rarebit
*2 oz butter*
*2 oz cheese*
*1¼ Spanish onions*
*2 slices hot dry toast*

*Peel onions and put in pan of boiling water with salt added, boil until tender one hour with the lid off. Then drain and chop fine, put butter and cheese in small pan and stir until mixture is blended, then add chopped onions, when all is hot through cut toast in squares and put a layer of toast at bottom of hot dish, then a layer of mixture. Repeat, leaving some mixture for the top. Serve hot. S and P.*

***Stewed Fish*** - sounds repulsive but once tried (and with good firm haddock) often repeated - unless you don't like white fish.

### Stewed Fish
*One cod or halibut steak, or fresh haddock*
*One ounce butter*
*2 oz flour*
*¼ pint water*
*¼ pint milk*
*One tablespoon chopped parsley*
*P and S*

*Stir until boiling. Wash and dry fish, put into pan and simmer gently 10 or 12 minutes, scald and chop parsley and mix with sauce. When fish is taken out of pan, pour sauce over fish.*

***Stewed Steak and Tomatoes.*** Good steak and onions make this welcome food, especially if you are a tomato fan. I am not. Tomatoes in my mother's recipes are always fresh and peeled, so this rather mixed vegetable dish should be worth the trouble. Be careful to pour the fat away. This sounds like a cookery class recipe, Miss Mosscrop demonstrating and talking, my mother getting the essentials on paper as fast as she could. I am sure she could already produce this good cut of shoulder steak, cooked in her mother's simple way long before Miss Mosscrop's day - and after.

### Steak with Tomatoes
*Steak for stewing, shoulder cut 1½ inches thick, one pound steak*
*One or two onions*
*One small carrot*
*One small turnip*
*1 pint stock or water*
*¼ lb tomatoes*
*P and S to taste*
*Little flour to thicken*
*1 oz dripping*

*Put dripping in stew pan and allow to get hot, put in steak with a spoon and slightly brown, turn and brown other side, remove steak and fry in the fat - two sliced onions. Pour the fat away, add small turnip, cut up tomatoes and put stock or water, stir till boiling, put in the meat, P and S and cover with a tight fitting lid, simmer one hour and ten minutes.*

### Pork Pie - a Raised Pie
A must. The recipe speaks for itself.
*¾ lb minced pork*
*Eighth pint of cold water to add to pork*
*One teaspoon salt*
*½ teaspoon pepper*
*A pinch of cayenne*
*10 oz flour, 4 oz lard*
*½ teaspoonful of salt*
*A good half teaspoonful of baking powder*
*1 pint boiling water*

*Put the flour on board and chop in lard, add salt and baking powder. Put in a bowl and add boiling water and work to a stiff paste. Keep it as hot as possible. Cut a piece off for the lid, roll a piece and line a greased tin. Put in the minced pork, line the edges and put on lid. Trim and decorate.*

*Pal, happily retired at the seaside.*

This reminds me of the pork and "tatty" pie, our unfailing traditional New Year celebration in our South Lancashire family and a very unfailing tradition in my mother's family. We were all involved except the youngest. When I was part of it I must have been about 10, which means about 1906. The tradition involved the pork and "tatty" pie and (for the elders) a pewter mug of ale - (if there weren't enough pewter mugs to go round one had a pottery mug instead) - sizzled by a red hot poker waiting between the bars of grandmother's kitchen fire. It made, I remember, a unique and lovely sound when immersed, a bit like the joyously impatient tapping of hailstones on our fanlight over the front door, "Let us in! Let us in!". But the pie was there, already prepared and perfect, kept hot in Grandma's stove in her kitchen range, and the mulled ale in its huge iron pan on the hob - a splendidly sensible Victorian arrangement, strong and sound into Edwardian New Years. Then we heard a distant and very clear gunshot: the clock chimed - it seemed impatient - as Grandma's tiny figure emerged from her armchair, a firm knock on her front door brought us to attention, also wound us up somehow: and Grandma hobbled slowly to the door. All the bells of heaven were bursting from the quiet town. We were all quiet then, the elders too: and Grandma's voice - very clear and sweet - called from the end of the lobby, "Who is there?" My eldest uncle - her first born - answered from without, "Ellis, Mother". He sounded glad, probably relieved his cold vigil was over. Then Grandma unbarred the door, "Come in, Ellis!" and "Happy New Years" swept into the world. Ellis swept his mother into a snowy embrace (it always seemed to snow in those winter days). He offered her the usual gifts, small indeed, but saying more - coal, shining ebony black, and bread (a crusty chunk), and a shining penny. Always the same through the years going by; little Grandma, Ellis's great arm guiding her all the way, bore the three gifts of our lives, and set them on the clean white sideboard among us while we kissed and "Happy New Yeared" one another. It was, I thought, being young yet old enough, a wonder - a secure miracle. And bells were still ringing in my new world. Midst all this comforting feel, I heard plates crackle, the empty table (scrubbed white) being overwhelmed with pies. I saw my mother cutting them, forks handed round, Grandma in her wooden armchair presiding - her pretty face a pink glow, very happy among her children - sons and daughters and a few of their children. I didn't know then how she was thinking of her Henry, gone ahead a few short New Years before. But we were there and we were allowed a sort of celestial sip from my father's larger mug of "mulled ale", and were glad of our slice of "Pork'n Tatty Pies". There must have been six or seven pies emerging from that hot oven and spread on the white kitchen table under Grandma's eye. And I saw, and was amazed to see, tears sparkling through her spectacles.

*Leigh Parish Church from the former railway embankment in Westleigh.*

### Pork 'n Tatty (potato) Pie

*Make a good short pastry; enough to line six or seven pie plates. For the filling proportions are more important than quantity. 2-3 lbs of best pork steak cut in small pieces and cooked slowly in a little water, but not too long. Only until it is tender.*

*Have ready a quantity of old potatoes and Spanish onions, also cooked and mashed together and add to the pork and mix. Add pepper and salt to taste (this means you must taste).*

*Judge the quantities of ingredients so that one flavour does not overcome another, especially the pork, which should be detectable.*

*Line the pie dish with fairly thin pastry. Fill generously with the pork mixture and cover with another, fairly thin lid of pastry. Always remember to moisten the edges of the pastry with a little water before putting on the lid, or they will not stick together. Make three little cuts in the top of the pie to leave the mixture room to breathe and prevent it overflowing in the oven. Cook in a moderate oven until pastry is cooked (30 to 40 minutes). Plates and forks should be ready for serving.*

On with the recipes. Very few were familiar, the result of the cookery classes and Miss Mosscrop (so it is enough to give **Newcastle Pudding** as it comes) but **barley water** must be welcomed with tumbrels and dances - a specific for colds in winter, feverish times and hot summers. And *"Cocanut Ice"* written and misspelt by me in 1913 and presented by the dentist's wife who eased my mother's yearly need in return for her recipe for bottling pears. It was an annual occasion but I don't think it was necessary. I think they enjoyed hobnobbing a bit. They were happy bottlers, those two women; but I did not like the dentist. He had an enthusiasm for crowning teeth, not a habit pleasing to a seventeen year old.

### Newcastle Pudding
*Put on a pan of water, prepare mould and lined greased paper.*
*2 oz butter*
*2 oz caster sugar*
*2 oz flour*
*2 eggs*
*Grated rind of ½ lemon, good teaspoonful*

*Cream butter and sugar, drop in one egg without beating, beat well, then add half of the flour; then the other egg, beat again, then the other half flour, grated lemon rind and last of all p and s. Put into mould and boil ¾ hour. Serve with raspberry sauce. Boil one oz sugar with ¼ pint of water 5 minutes. Then add juice of ½ lemon, one tablespoon of raspberry jam, strain and ready for use. You may thicken with arrowroot, ¼ teaspoon arrowroot with cold water, add arrowroot and boil for a few mins.*

### Barley water
*One oz boiled barley*
*Rind ½ lemon*
*One quart water*
*One 1¼ teaspoonful sugar*

*Wash barley in cold water, allow to boil 30 mins, strain off the water and add one quart of cold water, and lemon rind and the juice and simmer slowly one hour, strain and serve as required.*

### Cocanut Ice
*3 breakfast cups sugar*
*One cupful liquid (half milk and half water)*
*One cupful coconut (desiccated)*

### *Cocanut Ice (contin.)*
*Method. Place the sugar and liquid and half the coconut in a pan; bring to a boil and boil for 10 minutes. Remove from the heat and add the rest of the coconut. Beat for a minute or two; then pour into a wet tin. Dr. Peters' recipe 1913.*

Many names crowd in during these early 1900's and into the 1920's, and my mother's recipe swappers must have been legion: Miss Isherwood, Miss Calderbank, Miss Sherwood - all good solid north country names, and Miss Wilson, who brought parkin from Edinburgh and shared my first school ma'aming life with me in Liverpool. She was better, far, at it than I was ever - but she was Geography, I remember, and we shared 'digs' where light and heat were off when we marked papers after ten o'clock. We bought candles and moved elsewhere.

***Cod à lo Castolett*** uses patna rice, a new ingredient, evidently the cookery class and Miss Mosscrop's era moving into the 1914-1918 war.

### *Cod à lo Castolett*
*1 oz flour*
*2 lbs codfish*
*½ lb Patna rice*
*3 eggs*
*1 oz butter*
*½ pint milk*
*P, S and cayenne*
*Sprigs of parsley and cut lemon to garnish.*

*Pick the cod near the tail. Wash well and fold in muslin. Put in boiling water, to which has been added salt and lemon juice, boil 20 minutes. In another pan have boiling water. Add one tablespoon of salt and sprinkle in well washed rice and boil rapidly without lid until tender, about 15 minutes. When done, pour in a cupful of cold water, pour through a sieve, and place before bright fire, toss with two forks to dry. Put the eggs in cold water, boil ten minutes, then put in cold water. Blend butter and flour in pan, add milk gradually, boil 3 mins, add p and s and cayenne and finely chopped egg whites. Place cod in flakes, on hot dish, pour over, press yolks through strainer, to fall on sauce.*

I don't remember sampling this ever but if you can cope with "sprigs" of parsley and such in the meticulous detail of the Mosscrop style, it should turn into an enjoyable and not too expensive and exhausting a dish. I'm thinking that cod does need a bit of help - not the tastiest of fish left to itself. Try it.

*Lobster Cutlets.* Of this same era (cookery classes and what Lancashire then, as before and later, called Night School) we have Lobster Cutlets. I imagine our family smiling indulgently over this idea of my mother spending time on the thought of this - another exotic recipe we never tried, but had great fun hearing father read it, with mother amused and listening, murmuring - "not for us, really, Will, but it's something different." And Will "I like your own cookery best love, but let's have it in all the same. You might try it some day." So there is the impossibly expensive "tin of lobster", breadcrumbs, tablespoonful of cream, and the meticulous "rest" of the tasty oddment but we never got as far as tasting what I hope you will make. The instructions are logical and clear in Mother's generous pencil scribble - flowing and amused. So then the recipe:

### Lobster Cutlets
*One tin lobster*
*1 ½ oz butter*
*Lemon juice*
*Quarter pint milk*
*One teaspoonful lemon*
*One small teaspoon salt and fine grains of cayenne*
*One egg*
*1 ½ oz flour*
*One tablespoon cream*
*Some fine white breadcrumbs about ¼ pound*
*Some frying fat*
*¼ teaspoon pepper*

*Mince the lobster, put the butter and flour in saucepan, add the milk by degrees, then the cream and lemon juice, pepper, cayenne, mix thoroughly add the lobster, spread on a large dinner dish and allow to cool. When cool and firm divide cutlets into eight pieces. Beat the egg and paint over each cutlet. Then toss into breadcrumbs and fry in hot fat. P and salt mix in breadcrumbs.*

Many recipes of these times have names added to their titles, Miss Calderbank, Mrs. Sherwood - friends and recipe enthusiasts, long gone, for their **Verney pudding** (and please note the addition "serve with raspberry sauce". Whoever makes that now that the 21st century looms?)

Lobster cutlets

1 Tin lobster 1½ oz butter, juice
¼ pint milk 1 teaspoonful lemon
1 small teaspoon salt a few grains of cayene
egg 1½ oz flour. 1 tablespoon cream
some fine white bread crumbs about ¼ lb
some frying fat ¼ teaspoon pepper
Mince the lobster put the butter
and flour in saucepan, add the milk
by degrees then the cream lemon juice
pepper cayenne mix thoroughly add
the lobster, spread on a large
dinner dish and allow to cool,
when cool & firm divide into 8 parts cutlets
beat the egg and paint over each cutlet
then toss into bread crumbs and
fry in hot fat. & a salt mix in
bread crumbs

*Lobster cutlets, Gertrude Smith's handwriting.*

**Verney Pudding**
*Put on pan of water, prepare mould and paper.*

*One egg*
*Its weight in flour and butter (use half lard and half butter)*
*Weight of half the egg in caster sugar*
*½ tablespoon raspberry jam*
*¼ teaspoon carbonate of soda*

*Mode: cream butter and sugar, add the beaten egg, mix the flour and carbonate of soda and pass both through a sieve. Put in bowl and steam over the pan 1 ½ hours. Serve with raspberry or arrowroot sauce.*

**Polish stew** is also a museum piece, using lean beef steak (only ½ lb but certainly not cheap in 1914), pepper and salt to taste and a very small egg (a penny in those days was pretty lavish spending in a working household); but instruction is clear and you have 1 ½ lbs potatoes in good gravy.

**Polish Stew**
*½ lb beef steak*
*1 ½ oz beef suet*
*P and S to taste*
*1 ½ lbs potatoes*
*1 ½ oz onion*
*One very small egg*
*1 oz breadcrumbs.*

*Mince the beef, suet and onion, add p and s mix all together and form into a roll. Brush over with the beaten egg, and roll in the breadcrumbs. Put into a dripping tin, with ¼ pint of stock or water (boiling). Wash, peel and cut up potatoes, season with p and s; cook until the potatoes are soft. Serve with the roll in the centre of a dish and potatoes and gravy round.*

But now **Pea Soup** shines forth - cheap, common and nutritious marrowfat peas, especially if cooked with a pig's foot (a forefoot makes marrowfat a treat for the gods.) This is honest good eating though there are some who scorn it, as they pretend to be too superior to like tripe, although they have never tried it. "Ugh!" they shudder and cringe. But cooked, slowly boiled with lots of Spanish onions, and sauce made with good milk and cornflour - what the silly sneerers do miss - gastronomic glory!

*Mather Lane Bridge, Bedford, Leigh, the nearest crossing of the Bridgewater Canal to GB's home, with Mather Lane No.1 Mill on the left and Hall Lane Mill on the right.*

### Pea Soup

*Soak peas overnight, place in saucepan with ¼ lb lean bacon, or bones from roast beef, or fresh ones, and 3 pints of cold water, or the liquor in which some fresh meat has been boiled, a little salt and pepper. Place on a slow fire and simmer for 2 or 3 hours until the peas are sufficiently soft to run through and sieve. A piece of carrot or turnip and onion maybe added and a few celery seeds or celery tops. After running through sieve, repeat and serve with toasted bread.*

And **Beef Tea** - a simple, brief recipe involving, *"lean, juicy beef"*, salt (but not if for invalids) water, a pan, slow cooking, removal of any fat with paper (blotting). This "tea" hot and fresh, will save life, and restore feeblish health and create general well-being. It was one of my grandmother's legacies, and we who follow my mother give thanks for it. Grapple it to your heart. You will be forever blessed.

**Beef Tea**
*½ lb lean juicy beef*
*½ pint water*
*Pinch of salt, omit salt if invalid*

*Shred the meat with knife; put in jar with cold water, and salt, cover with buttered paper and allow to stand 2 hours. Put into pan of cold water, allowing the water to come within one inch of top of jar. Set over a gentle heat and bring slowly to boil and simmer slowly half an hour or an hour if time. Strain and remove any fat with paper.*

**Savoury omelet** is ornamental beyond need - too fussy for me - but there it is in all its glory - good eggs, but don't brown too far in your enthusiasm - remember the recipe says *"a nice brown."*

**Savoury Omelet**
*2 eggs*
*Onion chopped fine*
*½ teaspoon minced parsley, no stems*
*Pinch salt and pepper*
*Dust of sweet herb*
*1 oz butter*

*Butts Bridge over the Bridgewater Canal, Leigh.*

*Separate yolks; add to yolks salt, pepper, herbs, parsley and onion, stir together. Whip up the whites until stiff, stir them in lightly. Melt butter in omelet pan without browning it. Pour mixture in, place on gentle heat and fry a nice brown. Turn over place on hot dish and serve.*

Everyone can make Puff Pastry, my mother would say, yet here is her recipe; and do remember Rough Puff Pastry needs seven rollings, so be patient and perfect.

### Rough Puff Pastry
*½ lb flour*
*3 oz butter*
*3 oz lard*
*½ tsp lemon juice,*
*Cold water*

*Put the flour into a bowl, cut the shortening into pieces, about the size of nutmeg, moisten with the water and lemon juice, turn the pastry onto a board. Knead it up into one piece. Flour the board, and rolling pin, fold in layers, after rolling out, set aside in cool place ¼ hour, roll out and fold in 3 times, set aside ¼ hour again and repeat.*

*Make the night before if possible. Roll out and cut in squares, cut edges and fold over and brush with egg. Bake about 20 minutes The Rough Puff Pastry needs seven rollings.*

***Tapioca pudding*** also needs care and kindness otherwise it can hit back at you. Remember those unpalatable lumps?

### Tapioca Pudding
*2 oz sugar*
*2 eggs*
*1 pint milk*
*1 oz butter*
*A little grated lemon rind and salt*
*2 oz tapioca*

*Method: put the tapioca in pan with salt and milk, simmer slowly 20 mins, add sugar, lemon rind, yolks of eggs, and butter. Put in greased dish and bake in moderate oven ½ hour, whip up the whites and sweeten with tablespoon caster sugar, spread on the top of pudding. Make rough, dust with sugar, decorate with cherries and angelica and put in oven to brown.*

*Parsonage Colliery, Leigh, which had the deepest coal mine shaft and workings in the UK until the 1940's.*

**Swiss roll** - a worthwhile recipe which needs speed and dexterity in the making. My mother's instructions are all you need. Follow them and rejoice. Remember don't dally - get on with it.

### Swiss Roll
*3 eggs*
*3 oz flour*
*3 oz caster sugar*
*2 tablespoonfuls warm jam (see that the jam is ready warm)*

*Method: put eggs and sugar into a bowl, set over a pan of hot water and whisk 20 minutes. Sift the flour in, stir very lightly (do not beat after adding flour). Line a tin with greased paper and dust it over with caster sugar. Pour in the mixture spread it over the tin. Bake in moderate oven 6 mins. When done remove the paper, cut off the edges, spread with the warm jam, roll up as quickly as possible after it leaves the oven. Width of paper on oven shelf 9 x 14 ½ inches.*

## Malvern Pudding
*One pound fresh fruit*
*3 oz sugar or to sweeten*
*Slices of bread*

*Put the fresh fruit that's in season into a brass or enamel pan with the sugar,
let it stew until soft. Cut enough slices of bread to line a basin, cut off the
crusts. When the fruit is cooked, pour at once in lined basin, cover over with
bread. Put a plate on top place weight on it and let the pudding get quite
cold. Turn out on a dish, serve with custard or cream. This pudding should
be made the day before it is wanted. This is nicest made with redcurrants or
raspberries. Colour with cochineal.*

A specific "Mrs Horrocks' recipe" may not come amiss among satisfying
solids: prunes and senna powder, ginger and whisky. Taken alternate nights.
Need we say more? A simple indeed recipe.

## Mrs Horrocks' recipe
*1 lb prunes*
*1 lb sugar (syrup)*
*1 ½ oz senna powder*
*1 oz ground ginger,*
*2 tablespoons whisky*

*Stew prunes, remove stones and mix sugar, then senna and ground ginger,
then whisky. Take on alternate nights.*

**Coconut Macaroons** - usually favourites with old and young, and always
good with coffee at an evening party. Easy and presentable.
*¼ lb butter*
*¼ lb flour*
*3 oz caster sugar*
*3 oz desiccated coconut*
*2 eggs*
*½ teaspoon essence of vanilla*

*Cream butter and sugar, add yolks eggs and beat. Then one tablespoon of
sifted flour, then one tablespoon of coconut, then the whipped whites and
lastly the essence, drop in spoonfuls on a greased baking tin. Bake in hot
oven about 15 or 16 minutes.*

*Madeira Cake* A recipe culled at St. Thomas' Church sale. Church Bazaars happened once or twice a year and my mother made pin cushions stuffed with sawdust and with lace to ornament them. Quickly sold.

The recipe specifies Brown and Polson's Patent cornflour (2 oz) and Paisley flour (¾ oz) and 6 oz ordinary flour. Cornflour is a surer mixer than 'ordinary' flour - less likely to solidify into lumps. Follow this recipe carefully - note success depends on beating. Another truly rewarding exercise.

### Prize Madeira Cake
*2 oz Brown and Polson's 'patent' cornflour*
*¾ oz Brown and Polson's Paisley flour*
*6 oz ordinary flour*
*4 oz butter*
*5 oz caster sugar*
*3 eggs*
*Pinch of salt*
*¼ teaspoonful grated lemon rind, or a few drops essence of lemon.*

*Method. Measure out the ingredients. Butter a one pound cake tin. Beat the butter and sugar to a cream. Beat up the eggs well. Mix the ordinary flour and cornflour together. Add a little of the flour mixture to the butter and sugar, beating well, then a little of the egg, and go on repeating till both egg and flour are used up. Add the salt and grated lemon rind, and last of all the Paisley flour. Mix well and pour into the prepared cake tin. Bake for one hour in a moderately heated oven. When baked remove from the tin and lay on a wire tray to cool. The success of this cake depends mostly on the beating, which should be continued all the time the mixing is taking place.*

*Mrs Bibby's lemon cheese* is excellent. I like the last sentence. Mother writes as if listening to Mrs Bibby talk; she probably was.

### Mrs Bibby's Lemon Cheese
*3 lemons and the rind of 2*
*6 eggs*
*1 lb lump sugar*
*¼ lb butter*

*Heat sugar and butter first and melt slowly, then add the rind and juice and eggs. Stir well until it thickens, like honey. I have forgotten three tablespoons of cream together with the butter and sugar to melt.*

### *Lizzie's recipe from Bibby's*

Lizzie's husband, Seth, my mother's youngest brother, went to work at Bibby's cattle food factory in Liverpool, an adventure in those days. He wasn't a moneymaker (none of the family were) but a kindly soul. He died during grandmother France's lifetime.

***Jam tarts*** is easy and affords a pleasing little luxury.
*3 cups ground rice*
*1 ½ cups sugar*
*8 oz butter*
*4 eggs.*

*Beat butter to a cream add eggs then sugar and rice; mix well. Pastry first then jam and mixture last. Makes lovely tarts. Bake nicely.*

For the following years - another decade or so - many recipes are attached to names of friends or merely known by them as: ***Mrs Calderbank's Recipe*** *"good cheap pudding"* my mother remarks) or

*Bickershaw Colliery from the fields near Pennington Flash.*

**Mrs. Owen's Scones** and **G. Guest's Lemon Tart** all of which are evidently worthy the accolade and which now, sixty years and more later, can be followed easily and successfully as they are recorded by many family and friends' hands. My father's hand reappears in the 1920's, clear and neat, in **Kettlewell Biscuits** and **Queen Cakes**, and there is a gaggle of delicious sweetmeats (fudge especially) in our merry Irish schoolteacher's writing - whose home, with her bead-bonnetted mother, was not far away in our street.

### Kettlewell Biscuits
*2 cups flour*
*1 cup sugar*
*4 oz margarine*
*1 tsp salt*
*2 tsp baking powder*
*½ tsp carbonate soda in 2 tablespoons milk,*

*Roll out, cut and bake.*

### Queen Cakes
*¾lb flour*
*½ lb butter*
*½ lb sugar*
*4 eggs*
*¼ lb currants*
*Flavour to taste*

*Cream butter and sugar well together, add eggs one by one and beat well, sprinkle flour in whilst stirring, add currants and put in oven quickly.*

### Mrs Owen's Scones
*½ lb flour*
*2 oz lard or margarine*
*2 oz sugar or less*
*1 tsp baking powder*
*A little salt, and a good few raisins or currants according to taste.*

*Milk to mix, sour if in stock at the time, sufficient to make a soft dough, roll out and cut in cakes.*

### G. Guest's Lemon Tart
*Short pastry:*
*2 oz butter*
*4 oz flour*
*Pinch of B.P.*
*Cold water*

*Rub butter into flour: add B.P. and mix into stiff paste with water,
knead lightly and roll out once. Line tartlet tin or shallow pie dish.
Decorate edges.*

*Lemon mixture:*
*1 egg*
*Its weight in butter and sugar*
*1 oz savoy biscuits or bread crumbs,*
*Rind and juice of 1 lemon*

*Beat butter and sugar to a cream, add egg, beat all well. Add grated rind of
lemon and juice, and grated crumbs. Pour mixture into pastry case and bake
in moderate oven about ¼ hour.*

The years roll slowly by. Here come a spate of 1921 sweetmeats - between
the wars - in our Irish Annie Rabbit's even, schoolmistress hand. All very
detailed and precise. I like *"boil to 238 degrees"* for fondant mixture and
more the biblical ring of *"let bubbling cease"* reminding my generation of
a certain popular comedian (Stanley Holloway) who reported the command
of the Iron Duke to his assembled troops "Let battle commence". It was
considered amusing.

To return: Annie Rabbit's sweetmeats are crystal clear. Follow them and
you will be rewarded. ***Fondant Mixture, Everton Toffee***, this last interesting
as being made, not on a cooker - gas, certainly not at this 1920s time, nor
electricity - but on a coal fire *("remove from fire")*. ***Treacle Toffee*** -
remember that cream of tartar is essential: it balances any over-sweetness,
adds a pleasant pungency.

### Fondant Mixture
*3 lbs gran. sugar*
*1 tablespoonful of glucose*
*1 pint cold water*

### Fondant Mixture (contin.)

<u>Method</u>. *Put sugar and water in pan, dissolve, take off, stir in glucose. Replace and put lid on pan for a minute, then remove and allow mixture to boil to 238 degrees. Let bubbling cease. Pour into basin which has been previously rinsed in cold water. When partly cold beat with a wooden spoon.*

### Everton Toffee

*1 lb sugar*
*1 ½ gills water*
*3 oz butter*
*½ small teacup syrup*
*⅛ teaspoon of cream of tartar*
*Essence of lemon to taste*

<u>Method</u>. *Put the sugar, syrup, water and ⅓ butter into pan. Dissolve and boil, then add the cream of tartar, bring to the boil - boil to 260 degrees add the butter and boil up again to 300 degrees. Remove from the fire carefully add essence to taste and pour into well greased tin. When half cold mark into bars and when quite cold break. Store in a box which has been lined with parchment paper.*

### Treacle Toffee

*1 lb sugar (raw)*
*2 oz butter*
*3 tablespoonful of black treacle*
*3 tablespoons vinegar*
*3 tablespoons water*
*⅛ teaspoon cream of tartar*

<u>Method</u>. *Put sugar, treacle, butter, water, vinegar into pan - dissolve, add cream of tartar - boil about 10 minutes to 300 degrees or test by dropping a little into very cold water. Pour into a well greased tin and when set break up. Pack in box lined with parchment paper.*

**Miss Calderbank's recipe** is included now, a marginal note in my mother's hand as "**good cheap pudding**". Economy was the watchword as time rolled towards the second appalling war of 1939-45. Please realise this. Briefly the following "nice *cheap*" cakes rings the same bell.

*Mrs R. called us 'the Leppy family'* Annie Rabbit - Irish teacher in
- & with good cause. Manchester (Ancoats) - Lived
Peppermint Creams. with v. Irish mother (always
__Fondant Mixture__ wore a black bonnet)
in West St., Leigh
where we lived till
1921.

3 lbs of Gran Sugar. 1 tablespoonful of Glucose.
1 pt of cold water.
__Method__ Put Sugar water in pan.
dissolve. take off stir in Glucose.
Replace & put lid on pan for a minute
then remove tallow mixture to boil to
238°. Let bubbling cease.
Pour into basin which has been previously
rinsed in cold water - when partly
cold beat with a wooden spoon.

_____

Everton Toffee.
1 lb Sugar 1½ gills water 3 ozs Butter. ½ teacup small
Syrup ⅛ teasp of Cream of Tartar Essence of lemon black
__Method__ Put the sugar. syrup. water & ⅓ Butter into pan
dissolve & then add the cream of tartar bring to
the boil - boil to 260° add the butter & boil up
again to 300° Remove from the fire carefully

*Fondant Mixture and Everton Toffee. Annie Rabbit's handwriting with GB's
annotation.*

**Miss Calderbank's Recipe**
*1 cupful breadcrumbs*
*1 cup flour*
*½ cup suet*
*2 tablespoons treacle*
*½ top ginger*
*½ top carbonate soda*
*Milk to mix*
*(good cheap pudding)*

**Nice cheap cakes**
*¼ lb coconut*
*2oz flour*
*½ top baking powder*
*condensed milk*

We move on to **Christmas Cake** - Wilby's recipe, reproduced as he wrote it in capitals.

## CHRISTMAS CAKE
*1 LB BUTTER*
*1 LB SUGGAR*
*1¼ LBS FLOUR*
*1 LB PEEL*
*3 LBS CURRANTS*
*4 OZ ALMONDS*
*12 EGGS*
*1 TEESPOONFUL BAKING POWDER*
*LITTLE WHISKY*
*BAKE VERY SLOWLY 5 HOURS*
*ALMOND PASTE (INSIDE)*
*½ LB ALMONDS*
*¼ LB CASTOR SUGGAR*
*1 EGG*
*A FEW DROPS OF ESSENCE OF LEMON*
*A LITTLE SPICE*

Wilby Tickle became an analyst and supervised, with his own particular caring nature, the quality of the flour used in his mother's bakery in his native town where his younger brother was a doctor. I recall a rather

*Christmas Cake*

| | |
|---|---|
| 1 LB. | BUTTER |
| 1 LB. | SUGGAR |
| 1¼ LB. | FLOURE |
| 1 LB | PEEL |
| 3 " | CURRANTS. |
| 4 OZ | ALMONDS |
| 12 | EGGS. |
| 1 | TEESPOONFUL BAKING POWDER |
| | LITTLE WHISKY. |

BAKE VERY SLOWLY 5 HOURS

ALMOND PASTE (INSIDE)
½ LB ALMONDS
¼ LB CASTOR SUGGAR
1 EGG
A FEW DROPS OF ESSENCE OF LEMON
A LITTLE SPICE.

W. Tickle's.
(Wilbraham

{GB's note (1987) This recipe must have come in Wilby's writing after the 19/14 when I was married & living away from Leigh. My cousin had left school + was studying to be an analyst (chem.) working in his mother's confectionary business. He was a kind-hearted man ever. Very shy, philosopher. A good cousin — quiet humour, quiet life, thinker, not academic ; DV. Harry was his nearly twin, brother, much loved.

*Christmas Cake, Wilby Tickle's handwriting, with GB's annotation.*

dangerous custom (meant to be pleasant) when my cousins and I were young, in the early 1900s. For birthdays and other 'party' events a trifle appeared as a treat and in it were hidden surprises such as a well cleansed sixpence and an equally clean celluloid animal, very small but recognisable. Wilby was unlucky enough to find one - *something* - not trifle only, in his 6 year old mouth. Being trustful and courageous, he chewed on and on undaunted, till my mother realised the child's plight and rescued him from swallowing a battered celluloid doll. "Never again that sort of thing" was all she said, and never again it was. Trifle was enough - fresh sponge cakes plastered with raspberry or strawberry jam soaked in real egg custard and real whipped cream on top - was heaven of itself at any party we had to do with after that. What a child suffers when older hands think they can sagely "gild the lily". Poor Wilby! In his 'teens' he took to playing a drum (a pupil of the Manchester Hallé Orchestra's leading drummer) and practised at our grandmother's little house. Drums are hardly quiet instruments! The Baptist Church was adjacent to Grandma's, and one day a delegation waited upon her. "We are sorry, Mrs. France, but would you mind not playing your drum on Friday evening? - choir practice in church - a bit loud". So Grandma sweetly agreed to refrain, and still Wilby practised - but not on Fridays. She dearly loved sharing in our doings - kept our penny 'comics' under her sofa cushions for us! They were joyful visits. The 1920s now and here are some recipes from cooking friends of my mother's in Leigh.

**Bottled pears.** Advised if you are looking to keeping for future use. This recipe involved us in an annual expedition to our dentist's wife (an expert). I think it need not have happened, as the recipe is clear enough and never varied unless the pears required 'choosiness' according to the harvest. I imagine my mother and the dentist's wife enjoyed hobnobbing a bit. It went on for many years.

### Bottled Pears
*½lb lump sugar to 1 quart water. Boil to a nice syrup and let cool. Peel pears very smoothly and cut in two. Put in bottles and cover with liquid not quite to the top. Boil until it bubbles up well, like little silver balls. Let cool in pan, take out and screw up the lids.*

Then there's Miss Isherwood's gingerbread. (Do make this clear, straightforward, rewarding biscuit recipe *"cut into shapes"*). Excellent and not complicated. Try it.

### Miss Isherwood's Gingerbread
*½ lb syrup or treacle and syrup*
*½ lb sugar gran*
*¼ lb marge or butter*
*1 lb flour, tsp bicarbonate of soda*
*Tsp ground ginger*

*How? Syrup sugar butter melted together. Flour, ginger B.P. soda together well mixed. Mix gradually with wet mixture. Roll out and cut into shapes. Bake in moderate oven (middle shelf).*

### Shortbread
*1 lb flour*
*1 ½ lb butter*
*¼ lb white sugar*

*Mix into a paste and roll out about the thickness of an inch or so. Cut into squares or rounds, nip the edges with finger and thumb to form small points; ornament with a strip of candied peel in the centre and bake. It should be a pale lemon colour when done, not brown.*

Now **Mrs Drew's Coconut Ice**. Delicious. Another friend of my mother's at the old Leigh Parish Church where Grandmother France had been Warden and most of my family married and christened. Mrs. Drew used to make appliqué tea cosies for the church bazaars and made small egg cosies for our family as they grew from babyhood, after I moved from Leigh to Warwickshire.

**Coconut Ice** - *can be made with or without milk but it is nicer with milk.*

### Coconut Ice
*½ lb desiccated coconut*
*1 lb loaf sugar*
*small tea cupful of milk and ½ tsp carbonate of soda*

*Put the sugar and milk into a large enamelled saucepan, bring to the boil, stirring constantly to prevent burning. Let it boil for 5 minutes stirring rapidly. Then stir in the carbonate of soda. Take the saucepan off the fire and stir in the coconut. Pour half the mixture onto a tin lined with white paper. Colour the other half with cochineal and put on to the first layer. Level it with a knife or spoon and cut into bars when cold.*

We move to 1921 with *Mrs Mills' Coconut Biscuits*. A young, newly-wed came to live next door after my parents moved into a small town house in Bond Street, Leigh. Mrs Mills and my mother soon adopted one another happily as cooks and good neighbourliness and long lasting friendship followed.

### Mrs Mills' Coconut Biscuits
*1 lb desiccated coconut*
*½ lb and 1 dessert spoon caster sugar*
*2 eggs and a little milk*

*Mix well together and then press in eggcup dipped in cold water. Bake about 20 minutes until a golden brown.*

Next my mother's recipe for *Sultana or Currant Scones*. It's straightforward and sounds as if she is talking to me in homely fashion. After *"bake in rather hot oven about 10 minutes or more"*- "Your gas oven took 15 minutes all out to bake them nicely, so judge for yourself." It is truly typical of her friendly, mother to daughter manner. A *splendid scone*.

### Sultana or Currant Scones
*½ lb flour*
*2 oz butter*
*1 ¼ oz caster sugar*
*¼ pint of milk*
*1 ¼ top baking powder*
*Pinch salt.*

*Put flour, salt and baking powder into a bowl, rub in the butter, then add sugar and sultanas or currants and make into a stiff paste with the milk. Make into a round cake and cut across with knife and bake in rather hot oven about 10 minutes.*

*Recipe for anaemia* comes in two short lines. This was my mother's ailment over many years - bravely combated.

### Recipe for Anaemia
*Spinach juice and cream, carrot juice, beetroot juice and cream - all are good. Keep recipe handy - all ingredients should be readily available.*

**Potato cakes**
*6 oz plain flour*
*3 oz mashed potato*
*½ tsp salt*
*1 tsp cream of tartar*
*½ tsp bicarbonate of soda*
*Milk to mix*
*2 oz margarine (1941)*

*Mix dry ingredients. Rub in fat; stir in potatoes. Mix with milk to make dough - Hot oven 20-30 min. Potato cakes made with a beaten egg are good.*

Follow the recipe for potato cakes. They are a must. Have hot plate and fork, slice cake open and be lavish (if you can) with insertion of margarine or butter. Delicious. Some people top it with a poached egg. Not necessary to 'gild the lily'. Unless you're providing supper for a very hungry longing family. A mug of cold milk goes well with this as a meal. My mother adds a note. "Potato cakes made with a beaten egg are good". True, but the simple potato cake is good enough. Try it first.

**Potato Pie** is wholesome and satisfying and not expensive. Follow recipe with love and all will be well.

**Potato Pie**
*1 ½ lb pots*
*4 oz grated cheese*
*1 onion*
*2 tablespoons breadcrumbs.*
*1 pint milk and water or stock*
*Salt and pepper*

*Bridgewater Canal from Mather Lane Bridge, Bedford, Leigh.*

### Potato Pie (contin.)
*Boil onion with pots 5 mins. Strain well. Grease dish; layers pots, onion, breadcrumbs - cheese - leaving little fat and cheese for top. Season well, cover with layer of potato. Add liquid, cover with greased paper, and cook in slow oven till liquid is absorbed. Brown top under grill just before serving.*

**Chocolate Pudding**. Excellent - known as Brown Judd (and a special favourite of my sons) This recipe was sent to my old home, and welcomed us every time we went there, specially in cold weather. Very easy to make successfully if you follow the recipe as it is.

### Chocolate Pudding
*Cream 3 oz sugar and 3 oz butter. Break in 2 eggs. Mix well. Add rind (grated) and juice of one lemon. Mix 2 tablespoons choc powder with 4 oz flour and a pinch of B.P. and mix gradually with the rest, whisking mixture as you add flour. Steam one hour.*

**Apple Charlotte**. A 'different' result from Charlotte on top of apple. Acceptable to boys and very good too.

### Apple Charlotte
*4 oz flour,*
*4 oz butter*
*3-4 oz sugar*
*1 egg slightly beaten*

*Rub butter into flour and sugar. Add egg and knead. (I mix with a wooden spoon). Pat into shape in dish, making a case. Fill case with cooked apples and bake in pastry oven for ½ ¼ hr. If any egg is left brush pastry over with it.*

Mary's recipe for afternoon tea scones is excellent. The recipe is in Mary's handwriting, and reads:

### Mary's Afternoon Tea Scones
*2 breakfast cups of flour*
*Sugar to taste*
*Pinch of salt*
*5 heaped tea spoonfull [sic] of baking powder*
*1 table spoon butter melted*

### Mary's Afternoon
### Tea Scones (contin.)

*Mix all well, together [with] dry suet, with beaten egg & butter & about a breakfast cup of milk. Roll out & cut with a tumbler & bake in a quick oven for 10 minutes.*

Mary was my mother's servant (so Mary referred happily to herself - none of our family ever did). We respected her and we loved one another. She came to work with my mother when an aunt couldn't 'manage' her. She must have been fiftyish, and she and my mother (whose ways were patient and understanding) were happy together many years. I had gone afar and married, and used to "go home" to Leigh with my two boys who called the house "Mary's House". She lived in her own "back to back" little cottage, half a mile away and let herself in (her key) at 7.30 every day to spend her day with my parents for years. She had her aberrations which troubled, because she began at such times to talk wildly of well known local people- but a 'cuppa' tea with my mother put that right as soon as it started and, in the quiet of our little kitchen, sitting together and talking of pleasanter things, all was well.

Mary was in a choir (oratorio) and gave me her small splendid copy of "Messiah", inscribed with her name and my own 'new' one, after 1923.

Now we come to many blank pages and the end of my mother's book and her writing and my father's. The last page has a few addresses - purely personal to her, and then a 1939-1945 recipe for **Bee Syrup.**

In our house in Warwickshire, our family of four also housed a stranger - soon a friend - an artist and her family – a baby girl and two boys growing into school age. Mary's husband, also an artist, Stephen Bone, had been sent to Leamington as a camouflage

*Mary with Bill and EW (GB's sons) at 36 Bond Street, Leigh.*

artist in the War and shared lodgings with David Gentleman, another artist, but often joined our family - my mother, my sons and me in our cellar night retreat where I had transferred our family cot for the Bone baby who slept tranquilly in it, while as often happened, Mary and I slipped upstairs to our kitchen to cook a 2 a.m. early morning meal for the rest of us.

Mary and I took to keeping bees in our lovely garden; hence Stephen's recipe - the last in the recipe book. The years went by, my mother's 15 year widowhood began in 1939-40 at the turn of the year, soon my sons were serving in the R.A.F. and the Bone family moved back to their London home. We have been friends ever

*Portrait of Mrs Gertrude Smith (GB's mother, née France) painted by Stephen Bone.*

since; and that could be a long happy story. Bee syrup was made from my ration of sugar allowed for 2 hives. Here it is and ends the Recipe Book my parents began 50 years before.

### Bee Syrup
*10 lbs sugar*
*5 pints water*
*½ oz vinegar*
*½ oz salt*

*Boil a few minutes.*

# FAMILY TREE

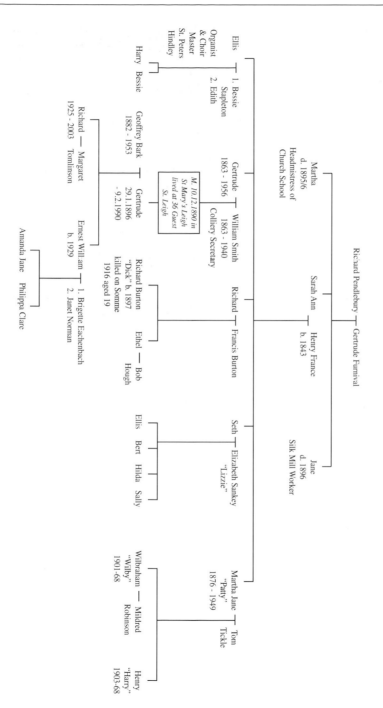

# INDEX OF RECIPES

*✳ Denotes a recipe which GB particularly recommends*

*(c) Vegetarian*

## IV. SWEET

*(a) Cakes & Biscuits*